The Amazing Common Sense Guide for Your Investment Success

The Amazing Common Sense Guide for Your Investment Success

The "Whole Investor" Approach for the New Millennium

John A. Thomchick

Writer's Showcase presented by *Writer's Digest*
San Jose New York Lincoln Shanghai

The Amazing Common Sense Guide for Your Investment Success
The "Whole Investor"Approach for the New Millennium

Published by Writer's Showcase presented by *Writer's Digest*
an imprint of iUniverse.com, Inc.

For information address:
iUniverse.com, Inc.
620 North 48th Street
Suite 201
Lincoln, NE 68504-3467
www.iuniverse.com

ISBN: 0-595-09874-6

Printed in the United States of America

To Evelyn and J.J.

Epigraph

If any young man expects without faith, without thought, without study, without patient, persevering labor, in the midst of and in spite of discouragement, to attain anything in this world that is worth attaining, he will simply wake up, by-and-by, and find that he has been playing the part of a fool.

M. J. Savage

Contents

"Absorb what is useful."

Bruce Lee

Preface

I use the phrase "Investment Impaired" in the first chapter of this guide and by so doing may give the impression that the text is concerned with political correctness. I confess to never having gotten overly caught up in that particular fad. On the other hand, I see no reason to insult people, some of whom find subtle distinctions in speaking and writing important. To this end, throughout the text, rather than get involved in he/she and his/her conventions, I use the second person "you" and "your." One interesting aspect of investing is that the financial markets do not care whether you are male or female, about the color of your skin, about your nationality of origin, or about life preferences you make. The markets do not care if you are physically impaired. The markets will gladly take your money without regard to any of these considerations.

The first objective of this guide is to help you determine whether you should even be an investor. I try to help you in this exercise in Chapters 1-2. If you decide, indeed, that you should be an investor, this guide is further intended to help you evaluate various investment classes. In Chapters 2-9, I introduce a number of financial markets and their corresponding investment vehicles. In Chapters 10-13 and the appendices, I cover related investing topics.

Sometimes, if you give the markets their due respect, they will return your money and in some cases even give you a profit. A second objective of this guide is to instill in you a respect for the markets, so that you can, indeed, profit from them. Gaining respect for the markets begins with a thorough examination of ourselves.

Please note that nothing in this guide is intended as specific investment advice. Specific advice can be given only after a thorough study and understanding of an individual's peculiar circumstances. Some investments will be appropriate for some investors and inappropriate for others. **All investment decisions are ultimately the responsibility of the individual investor.** Also always keep in mind that past results, be they successes or failures, are not necessarily indicative of future results.

J.A.T.

Acknowledgements

I want to thank my brother, Jerry Thomchick, renowned investor, who kindly read every word of this guide and usually agreed with what I had to say. My wife, Evelyn, also helped to edit several sections. And just so all this evaluation was not in the family, Joe Filko, a long-time friend and critic read the chapter on life insurance. A big "thank you" to each of you.

Chapter 1

Making the Investor Whole

"That money talks I'll not deny
I heard it once, it said good-bye."

Anonymous

Why Should You Believe Me?

Will Rogers commented that economists know as much about the economy as anybody else. I've invested in most well-known financial instruments, so I might argue that I know as much about investing as anybody else. But that would be a *non sequitur par excellence, in totidem verbis*. All right, I promise no more foreign or ancient languages—that's not me. I could have entitled this section "Why you *should* believe me"—but that's not me, either. Instead, I prefer to gain your trust gradually.

What I can offer you is experience. I believe I can save you from some of the mistakes I've made. I can also direct you to some of the best references and investing techniques. I note that I've made money on all financial instruments I've invested in. I've also lost money in most of the financial instruments I've invested in. Anybody who tells you they've never lost money in their investments is either very, very lucky or else a liar. The real trick is to make more money than you lose.

In fact, before I go on, in the very next sentence I'll give you the most important lesson in Investing 101. It is simply: **Cut your losses fast.** Easy to say, much more difficult to implement. It took me a long time to learn this rule, and even today I have difficulty with it. We live in a society where the emphasis is on winning. Dick at the office will gladly tell you about that stock that doubled in price, but does he tell you about the one that went down 50%? It is precisely the discipline of cutting these latter investments long before they become 50% losers that will make you an investment winner.

A little about me. I have a Ph.D. in physics. I have not done any serious physics since 1985. Some people could argue convincingly that I've never done any serious physics. What I could argue from my experience is that many Ph.D.'s in physics or any other subject don't know how to make money. Since 1985 I've done a lot of investing, unfortunately right through the stock market crash of 1987. Many financial advisors and newsletter gurus claim they told their clients to get out of the market before the crash, and some even claim to have made tons of money for their clients during the crash. I make no such claims. I lost money during the great crash of 1987, somewhere in the neighborhood of $8,000, which was a hefty fraction of my discretionary (investment) funds at the time. I was in London, England on the actual day of the crash, Monday, October 19. From the London newspapers one would have actually expected to see bricks and mortar littering the streets of The City, London's financial district. I later read that Peter Lynch, the head of Fidelity's Magellan Fund at the time, was in Ireland the same day—having kissed the blarney stone, some luck that—and that his fund indeed took a big hit. So I felt that I was in good company, being away from the markets that day, though it never allowed me to suffer my monetary loss any less. I will say, though, that that single day, October 19, 1987 was one of the most influential motivating factors in my subsequent detailed study of investments and the financial markets.

This guide is a compilation of my investment experience. It is not intended to be comprehensive. Neither is it intended to give investment advice, which must be tailored to an individual's particular circumstances. Rather this guide is intended to educate, to give you in one convenient place some of the best financial references for additional reading, and to give you a variety of addresses so you can obtain additional information. It is also intended to prepare you for the day when the 1990s-2000 Great Bull Market in stocks has finally run its course. All markets move in cycles, though these cycles tend to be very asymmetrical. There are many other things besides stocks to invest in, and, as one of the overriding themes in this guide is diversification, we will introduce you to some different investment possibilities.

Finally this guide is intended to make you aware of the various financial markets, to make you aware that they are interrelated, and convince you that you should pay attention to them. This guide will help you get started. Along the way perhaps I can poke some holes in a few investment myths and occasionally even amuse you for your effort.

This guide will not be a favorite among financial planners or investment advisors (let's call them financial advisors). The reason is that I want you, the "whole" investor, to gain enough confidence about investing to eschew forever financial advisors. I'm not arguing here that financial advisors are good, bad, sincere, crooked, honest, cheats or anything else. Some indeed are bad, crooked or cheats, but most are ethical people like you or me trying to make a living. Some are glorified insurance salesmen who sell mutual funds on the side. The problem is that they make a living from the investor by providing services that you could easily be performing yourself, maybe performing them much better than they do. After all, the typical financial advisor will have many clients to look after, so how much attention can he possibly be devoting to your account? Will he give it as much care as you would? Does he have as much concern about your money as you do? Mostly these guys have a formula they follow. "How about this mutual fund? It went up 35% last year and its front end load is only 5.75%." Now 35% per year sounds pretty darn good, even in the Great Bull Market. So you say, "Yeah, let's do that," and you've lost 5.75% of your money before you even get invested (see chapter on Mutuality). Part of that 5.75% goes into the advisor's pocket.

Note that there is a difference between financial advisors, who are mostly salespeople, and professional money managers. In the following chapters I will point out some opportunities with professional money managers. Such people study the markets, know the in and outs of investing and typically make their money by taking a percentage of the profits they earn for the investor. Thus, they have a vested interest in seeing that your investments do well. To my way of thinking, you are far better off paying this kind of person rather than the kind who takes a fee for selling you a product that you could easily buy yourself.

The Investment Impaired

My experience is that few people are satisfied with their investing results. Some have unrealistic expectations, but most simply to not practice the simple, common sense principles I outline below. I refer to these people as the "Investment Impaired." Maybe your next question should be: "Am I one of these people?" My quick answer is: "You very likely may be one of the investment impaired, even if you've been investing for a long time." Most people are too busy with their livelihoods, their families or their hobbies (golf comes to mind) to really delve into the investment world. My wife is a good example. She is extremely busy with her career and doting on our son, so she lets me do all the investing. (She *is* impressed on those days when the Dow moves up or down a couple hundred points, however.) She reads several business newspapers, keeps up with currency valuations, freight indices and supply-chain management practices because she teaches international logistics. But investing? No way. For most people, though, there usually comes a day when they wish they had paid more attention to their investments and to investing in general. Whether you've reached that point in your life or not, this guide can help.

Maybe a more pertinent question than the one posed above is "Should I be an investor in the first place?" The answer to this question revolves around what I will call discretionary money and which I will define as money you could afford to lose without it affecting your lifestyle. If the only money you have will eventually be needed to repair a leaky roof or to purchase a new furnace, then that is not discretionary money. If the nest egg you've saved is intended to send the kids through college, then that is not discretionary money. I know, I know—a lot of mutual fund profits from the 1980s and 1990s ended up on housetops, in basements and at university treasuries. If this is true in your case, allow me to say that you were lucky. As I write this in early 2000, we are long overdue for a bear market (i.e., a pullback of >20%) in the major stock averages, so I have this ugly feeling that there will yet be a generation of prospective college students who will see their tuition money significantly eroded. It seems to be common knowledge that many people have even taken out second mortgages or borrowed using their credit cards in order to get into this wild stock market. But borrowed money is not discretionary money. Many will disagree with me, but money that is not discretionary money should only be placed in the safest of financial instruments, such as money market accounts or bank CDs.

This brings me around to another subject that I feel very strongly about, namely debt. I'm referring here to personal debt. You may feel that you have discretionary money, but if you are in debt, especially in serious debt, then that money may not be discretionary at all. You may have a very high income and feel that you have your debt payments under control. But imagine what would happen if that situation were to change? I've seen it happen to acquaintances. Debt can crush you.

Most people's major debt is their mortgage. People even "buy up" to increase their mortgage and, hence, the deduction on their income tax return. Does this really make sense? Suppose for sake of argument (and round numbers) that you pay $10,000 per year in mortgage interest payments. The lending institution graciously accepts this $10,000, not one penny of which goes to decreasing the principle amount of your loan. Now, next April your accountant puts down on Schedule A that you paid $10,000 in mortgage interest. Let's suppose for sake of argument that you are in the highest tax bracket, 39.6% on 1999 returns. If your deduction is not limited, then you can argue that you effectively get back $3,960. Actually, you would have had a standard deduction even if you hadn't itemized, so this is a bit of a fake, but let's assume the standard deduction is already covered by state and local taxes, plus charitable and miscellaneous deductions. So the result is that you pay $3,960 less in taxes than you would have without the mortgage interest expense, and you feel very gratified. But have you gained anything monetarily? No. You've lost $6,040, or 60.4% of the mortgage interest, upon which you will never receive any return and, for that matter, never see again. If your tax bracket is only 28% then you lose $7,200 or 72% of the mortgage interest payment. My suggestion is that if you think you have discretionary money and you are paying mortgage interest payments, use the imagined discretionary money to pay off your mortgage. Once you no longer have that mortgage interest payment you will have that extra $6,040 to $7,200 a year to put into a truly discretionary account.

I'm not saying that debt has no place in our modern society. Few businesses would get started, few homes would be purchased without it. What I am suggesting is that you should pay off that debt as soon as possible and don't pretend that you have investing money when you are throwing equally good money down the mortgage interest payment drain. This myth of having to buy up to increase your mortgage deduction benefits both the banking and real estate industries, but it sure doesn't benefit your bottom line. When you take into consideration the higher real estate taxes and the higher cost of upkeep, many people would be far better off in smaller houses. If you can pay cash, then flaunt it. It you have to borrow, reconsider.

Earl Nightingale told the story of a father who while reading a newspaper was interrupted by his little boy. To give the youngster something to do, the father seeing a picture of the world on one page tore up the advertisement into small pieces and suggested to his son that he put the world together again with some Scotch tape. Somewhat to the father's surprise the little boy brought back the puzzle all completed in about five minutes. The father asked his son how he had finished so quickly. "Well, Dad," said the boy, "you see there was this picture of a man on the other side. I just put the man together and the world came out okay."

Allow me to suggest that if we can put the investor together, his world will come out okay. In this guide I'm going to say things that many people simply do not want to hear. My pontifications above on mortgage debt is a good example. Many people simply want the status of a larger house in an upscale neighborhood, or the status of a second house in the mountains or at the shore. If you have the money for these things, fine. Most people don't. They have to get a mortgage. If this is you, then you have been brainwashed by the banking and real estate industries. The word "upscale" itself is nothing more than brainwashing.

Saying things that people don't want to hear is sometimes the best medicine. I've learned far more from books that said things I didn't agree with than from those that agreed with every aspect of my comfortable existence. Many times that slash of cold water in the face is good for us.

In the rest of this chapter, let me begin putting the investor together—making the investor "whole." This revolves around the topics of temperament, knowledge, diversification and money management. I won't keep beating on the debt horse, only simply say: "First get out of debt." The chapters following this one will begin a discussion of the investor's world.

Temperament

Investors are individuals with all the attendant varied experiences and emotional make-ups. Not all investments are equally suitable for every investor. Some investors will be satisfied with the most conservative investments while others will enjoy the wild ride of the futures market where fortunes can be literally made or lost within days, sometimes even hours. The usual test is whether the investment you've chosen allows you to sleep at night. Some of the knowledge you will gain from this guide will allow you to sleep better with your investments. But if you cannot sleep at night worrying about an investment, you should get out of it.

Worrying about investments has another nasty side effect, other than not being able to sleep. It can dramatically affect your bottom line. If you worry over the slightest adverse move in your investments you could end up trading too much. This has the result of piling up too many commission charges as well as the possibility of missing dramatic moves in your favor. Personally, I've had the opposite problem of not trading often enough, but rather of sticking with an investment through thick and thin. This can have adverse results, too, and I'm gradually working through this difficulty in my personal trading.

I believe temperament can be modified, as mine has been with my infrequent trading. Extending your knowledge of investing and the investing markets will help, as will diversification of your investment assets and your awareness of money management techniques applied to your investments. Nevertheless, there might be investments that you are comfortable with, others that you are uncomfortable with, some that you simply enjoy being in, while others you just hate. That is fine. Don't invest in things you are uncomfortable with or in things you dislike. Generally speaking, there are enough investments out there that even the most conservative investor can still diversify.

Knowledge

In early 2000, what with all the financial publications, investment books, newsletters, television financial news shows and the Internet, lack of information is not the problem. The real problem is information overload. I readily admit that my biggest problem in investing is having the time to sift through all this information, and maybe more importantly, having the time to digest it. It is a problem that you will have to face and cope with. It is not trivial. On just about any investment subject, be it interest rates, stock market direction, inflation, or whatever, on any given day I can get convincing, conflicting arguments on either side of the issue.

One pet peeve I have is the guest market analysts on CNBC who come on and explain the stock market rise by stating that "the market climbs a wall of worry." The commentators usually respond with an approving stare that implies, "Wow, this guy's really smart." But what does this really mean? They go on to state that nearly everyone is worried, so the bull market is on track—then everyone around the table breathes a sigh of relief. I know what they mean. They mean that as long as investors are worried, there still remains some caution in buying and so the market hasn't yet reached manic heights. But have they really imparted some snippet of great wisdom? If liquidity in the country dried up and the last trickle of money came into the mutual fund coffers, or if investor psychology turned bearish due to war or famine or pestilence, then even if every investor in the market was worried (and they probably are every day), would the market climb higher? I don't think so.

The point is that as investors we really have to separate what is important from what is nonsensical. In the investment world there are a lot of clichés based on half-truths that are not important. In the short space I have here, I cannot list and protect you from all of them. But if you hear something that sounds a little strange or that you don't understand, don't just accept it—it's probably half-baked or plain wrong. Begin to analyze things for yourself. Your common sense will usually win out.

Just where does the whole investor begin? For general information read one or more of *The Wall Street Journal, Investor's Business Daily, Barron's* or *The Economist.* Here again is where the investor's temperament comes into play. *The Wall Street Journal* and *Investor's Business Daily* publish five days a week, while *Barron's* and *The Economist* are weekly publications. Some people will be satisfied to keep up with their investments and business news on a weekly basis, while others will want to keep abreast daily (and others hourly). Some will like *Investor's Business Daily* crammed full of detailed stock tables and charts, others will prefer *The Wall Street Journal's* more extensive feature articles and expanded commentary. Those who want a more international outlook will like the London based *The Economist* which, however, does not list any stock prices. Also you will not go wrong with *Business Week* or two newer financial magazines, *Worth* and *Bloomberg Personal.* The addresses and telephone numbers are listed at the end of this chapter.

Learn as much as you can about an investment before you make the plunge. You will never learn everything there is to know and this need not lead to inaction. There are analysts at major brokerage houses who spend their full time researching a specific company or a specific investing sector, and they don't know everything there is to know. But general information is readily available. If you are buying the stock of a company, know what business the company is in. Find out about the company's earnings the past several years and the past several quarters. Find out whether they are paying dividends or plowing money back into research and development. Take a look at the historical price chart. Where are the historical highs and lows and the areas of support (defined in Chapter 10) for this stock? Find a more recent price chart. Has the price been rising, falling or flat? Who is the company's competition? Is that sector of the economy hot, slow or neutral?

In addition, take the time to know what the general marketplace has been doing. Are stocks as a whole moving up or down in price? Are interest rates favorable or unfavorable? Is inflation a concern? Are commodity prices affecting my company's stock? Is there impending legislation or political considerations affecting the stock?

No investment can be viewed in isolation from other investment sectors. A recurring theme of this guide will be that investment sectors are interrelated. Some go up in price together, others go in opposite directions. As you read through this guide and begin investigating markets on your own, I predict that you will find these interrelations a fascinating subject.

And keep in mind, that in investing, as in any other worthwhile field, education is an ongoing endeavor. Most of the investing concepts you learn will remain immutable, but new information arrives daily.

Diversification

I know a financial advisor right in my hometown who believes that diversification is splitting your investment portfolio into four high growth U.S. stock funds. From such depths of confusion is where the expression "Don't confuse brains with a bull market" springs forth.

By diversification I mean splitting your discretionary money up among investment classes and within those investment classes splitting up your money into different sectors or categories. I will not suggest here any specific ratios for dividing up your investment assets because again this depends on an investor's temperament and comfort zone. Besides I suggest some flexibility in these ratios if a certain investment class is outperforming and growing rapidly. In that case you might want to leave the money where it is rather than constantly reallocating. But if you have 85% of your portfolio in gold coins, then you are overweighed in that area. If you have 85% of your portfolio in stocks, you are over-weighed in stocks. If your normal weighting in stocks is 30% of your portfolio but this investment class grows to where it is 35-40% of your portfolio, I wouldn't necessarily reallocate funds. If it grows to a much higher percentage, you might take profits and reinvest them in other parts of your portfolio.

I also note that just because you have decided to put 30% of your portfolio in one investment class, such as stocks, if you own only technology stocks then you are overweighed in tech stocks. Also just because you've allocated a certain amount of money to a particular investment class does not mean that the entire amount has to be invested all the time. For example, in your stock portfolio it may be prudent to keep some of your powder dry (probably in a money market account) in the event that a bargain comes along. Also there may be those occasions when it is wise to take profits yet inappropriate to reinvest that money in another stock. However, even if the money is not actively invested in that class I still consider it in that class—and so should you.

The reason for diversification is simply prudence. Though I will try in this guide to prepare you for shocks, there is always the chance that a particular investment class will encounter a sudden downturn. If you just happen to have all or most of your discretionary money in that market during this downturn, the blow could be devastating. However, if your money is divided into many investment classes, the downturn in one class will represent much less of a blow to your overall portfolio. It is very unlikely that all investment classes would experience a downturn at the same time, and while one is down another may even outperform during that period.

Money Management

Money management has as much to do with discipline as with how to divide up your money or how to keep a watch on it. I believe this is the most important aspect of becoming a whole investor and it is the most difficult to master. Many emotions are involved and pride plays a huge role. I believe if you truly mastered this aspect of investing that you could even get away without much diversification or for that matter without much knowledge of what you're investing in. But I wouldn't try it. Even professional investors have difficulty with the money management aspect of their trade, so you should not think, even if you've applied the strictest discipline in other areas of your life, that you will easily learn it.

The first aspect of money management you have to struggle with is how, in fact, to divide up your discretionary funds. Temperament and your knowledge of the different investment classes will naturally come into play, and as you gain experience you may even decide to allocate some money to entirely new investment classes. This happened to me when after some significant study and paper trading (trading without using actual money), I decided to open a small commodity futures trading account. I must be honest—I ran this first account into the ground, mostly because I did not apply solid money management practices. After some soul-searching and additional study I opened a second account at which I've done better if not spectacularly. If you're just starting out and have not studied the futures markets, you definitely do **not** want to allocate money to a commodity futures account.

You will have to make some decisions and start somewhere. Allocate your money to at least four or five different investment classes. Equal amounts do not have to be in each account, but that certainly would be one way to start. If the analogy works for you, imagine the money in separate envelopes or files. Money from one envelope should not be commingled with money from another envelope. Please note that merely allocating money to these different classes does not mean that that money has to be immediately invested in those classes. Money can always be held in reserve, usually earning interest in a money market account, CD or t-bill while it waits for a bargain to become available in that class.

Initially, all your money, in all investment classes, will be in the form of cash. So what's the big deal? If it's all in cash anyway, why do you have to play this allocation game? This is where discipline comes into play. The great run in the U.S. stock market in recent years provides a great example here. You know you should be diversified, but you see the stock market going up almost daily, resulting in astonishing yearly returns. Greed blurs your thinking. (Greed is a sneaky, cowardly killer of discipline). Why not put all your money into stocks? With such great returns this seems like a no-brainer. But is it prudent? In about a six week period in 1987 the Dow Industrials sank from over 2700 to near 1600, approximately a 40% decline. Many individual stocks and mutual funds declined even more. Should you expose your entire portfolio to this kind of risk? Losing 40% of a portfolio would be a major blow. It might even cause you to eschew investing forever. But while losing 40% of a quarter of your portfolio (i.e., 10% of your total portfolio) would still be upsetting, you could survive it—and live to do battle another day.

I know I'm spending a lot of time on this seemingly simple concept, but in order to put the investor together, I must emphasize this money management point. You can see that this concept cannot be separated from temperament, knowledge and diversification. What distinguishes it is the discipline required and the most important aspect—survival. You could have a great investment temperament, gain all kinds of investment knowledge and even totally believe in diversification, and still not survive this sometimes brutal investing game.

Begin by dividing that discretionary money up into four or five investment classes. Do not overweight one or two. Only experience will give you a firmer grasp of the exact percentages you ultimately want in each. Balance should always be the key. If one of your investment classes increases in value dramatically, then certainly allow it to hold a higher percentage of assets. If, however, it begins to dominate and forces your portfolio out of balance, then take some profits and sow them into your other investment classes. This is the part that will take some discipline—and where greed comes into play.

Another difficulty that can affect balance and survival is when one of your investment classes declines in value. Friends and especially brokers can convince you this is the time to reallocate and dump more money into that investment class. Aren't you supposed to buy when prices are low, and isn't your portfolio out of balance anyway because of this decline? I urge caution. This may be the exact wrong time for reallocation of funds. You may be far better off getting out of the investment altogether. Markets and investment classes decline in value for some reason, just as markets and investment classes increase in value for a reason. Make certain you grasp what's causing the decline (knowledge). You will most often be better off waiting until that investment bottoms out and begins increasing in value again.

Which brings me back to the most important lesson of investing 101, namely, cutting your losses fast. At first blush, this may seem like exactly the wrong thing to do. After all, when an investment decreases in value, isn't it much more of a bargain? Wouldn't it be better to double up on the investment after it falls 10 or 15%? Besides, this is the time when pride comes into play. (Pride is another devious killer of discipline.) We hate to admit that we made an investment mistake, even to ourselves. Hope, which should have no place in the investor's range of emotions, convinces us that the investment will surely turn around and regain its former value. If only we buy more now we can get out at the original value with a small profit. Well, let me be blunt. This is wrong-headed thinking. Don't compound your losses by buying at a lower price. **Cut your losses fast.**

How fast? Oh, boy—I wish I had a secret formula. This decision has less to do with temperament than it does with the investment class and the volatility of the particular investment. Take stocks as an example. Suppose you decide that a 10% loss is the maximum you will tolerate, a very reasonable decision. A $20 stock would only have to decline two points and you would be out of there. That's fine. On 100 shares you would lose $200 plus commissions, but you had the discipline to stick with your decision.

On a $70 stock your program would allow the stock to drop 7 points before you would sell. On 100 shares you would lose $700 plus commissions. This may be more of a loss than you should rightfully accept. A better program might be to accept losses up to a certain percentage of your portfolio, or better yet up to a certain percentage of the amount allotted to that investment class. Suppose you have allocated $10,000 to your stock portfolio, and you decide you can tolerate a 3% portfolio loss, or $300, on any given trade. Then you could have allowed the $20 stock to drop to 17, but the $70 stock could only drop to 67.

As you can see there is no one way to accomplish your objective, but you must choose how you will exit your losses and stick to it. Discipline is the key! In the above example if that $70 stock were a high growth technology company, the $300 loss limit or 3 points on 100 shares might be too tight a limit for you to remain invested for very long. The share prices of technology stocks are very volatile and the stocks are aggressively bought and sold. This is where temperament, knowledge and diversification come in. You cannot separate them from the money management aspect. After some trading experience you may decide that you are more comfortable with $20 stocks and that they fit in better with your diversification and loss limit programs.

Note that the loss limits on different investment classes can vary substantially. I would accept no losses on the money market, CD and insurance portions of my portfolio, but I might accept a 25% loss on my rare coins because these are items that I've decided to hang on to. In general, for those investments that are readily tradable I recommend accepting losses of from 5% to no more than 15%. There are just too many investments out there to be holding onto losers for very long.

If you have a winner you can slide your loss limit along with the price increase. Though you should allow your winning investments to run, never be ashamed or afraid to take profits. If you are using a 10% loss limit, when your $20 stock moves up to $30 allow it to go to 35 or 40 if it wants to, but if it retraces 10% or 3 points to 27, don't be afraid to sell.

Sure, you missed the opportunity to sell it at 30, but you also might have saved yourself a lot of self-incrimination when it falls to 24. If it looks strong again at 25 or 26 you can always get back in. The main point is that you had the discipline to follow your program and in the long run that's going to be more important than those three points you missed.

Conclusion

Following some simple, common sense principles can lead you to investing success. Even the investment impaired can be made whole and lead productive investing lives. No claim is made that this is easy, but the process can be interesting and fun. The first test is whether you should be in the investing game in the first place. This requires discretionary money, money that is not needed for emergencies or for long term family plans, money that if lost would not substantially affect your lifestyle. Investing implies risk and, at the minimum, tying up assets for extended periods, so money that is not discretionary should be placed only in the most conservative, liquid instruments.

If you do have discretionary money, learn what your investing temperament is. If an investment will not allow you to sleep at night, then get out of it. Know what you are investing in. Take the time and effort to learn about the specific investment and also the market conditions of the general investment class. Never invest in anything you have no knowledge of. Divide your discretionary money into several investment classes. This will substantially reduce your exposure to any one class and allow you to survive in times of adverse market conditions. Apply prudent money management techniques to all your investment decisions. Do not overweight your portfolio in one investment class, nor in any one sector within that class. And finally, cut losses fast. Choose discipline over pride. There are too many investment opportunities to be wasting time with losers. Finally, let your winners run but never be afraid to take profits.

In the remainder of this guide I will be introducing many investment classes and sometimes will give references and names of vendors. I note that as of this writing, I am completely independent of any brokerage house or other financial institution. On the other hand, I will not hesitate to tell you when I've had a good experience with one or the other.

Addresses

The Wall Street Journal
200 Liberty St.
New York, NY 10281
(800)-JOURNAL
www.wsj.com

Investor's Business Daily
12655 Beatrice St.
Los Angeles, CA 90066
(800)-831-2525
www.investors.com

Barrons
200 Liberty Street
New York, NY 10281
(212)-416-2000
www.barrons.com

The Economist
111 West 57th St.
New York, NY 10019
(212)-541-5730
www.economist.com

Business Week
1221 Avenue of the Americas
New York, NY 10020
(800)-635-1200
www.businessweek.com

Worth
575 Lexington Ave.
New York, NY 10022
(800)-777-1851
www.worth.com

Bloomberg Personal
100 Business Park Drive
Skillman, NJ 08558
(800)-731-5005
www.bloomberg.com

Chapter 2

Budgets and Banking

The starting point of all achievement, Definiteness of Purpose
—knowing what your goal is, knowing what you want—fills you
with a success-consciousness and protects you against failure.

Napoleon Hill

Your Goal Should Be Budgeting—for Success

Planning and budgeting are an important component of any investment
strategy. You may already have the funds with which you plan to diversify
into various investment classes. Whether this is true or not, this chapter
will be useful in helping you find extra discretionary money to put into
your investment portfolio. When I talk about planning and budgeting
some people may get images of costly computers and abstruse software
manuals. If you have a computer, fine—software in this area is very user
friendly. But all you really need is a tablet and pencil…okay, and maybe a
folder. I talk first about a monthly budget, then lead you through a
longer-range plan.

Banking can be an important part of a budget and longer term planning. Almost everyone needs a bank for checking and savings accounts,
credit cards, ATM-cards, safe deposit boxes and so on. Banking fees

have been on the increase. It is important to find a bank where you receive excellent service for a reasonable price. A good bank can also be the source for a conservative portion of your investment portfolio.

Monthly Budgets

You may be paid or receive income on a different time frame than a monthly basis, but the discussion here should be readily transferable to your individual situation. When you are paid, you may cash a check or have funds transferred directly into a checking account. Regardless of the method, it is important before you start spending, that you know where that money is going. It is my personal opinion, based on causal observation of friends, acquaintances, even strangers, that many people do not take great care in the disbursement of their hard-earned money. Of course, my reputation is that of a tightwad, but maybe if more people adopted my attitude they would have more money to invest.

I'll give you a few examples. I'll bet that many people, unless they use a credit card every time they fill up, do not know how much they spend on gasoline for their cars every month, or how much on car repairs. Many people probably don't know how much they spend on workday lunches for a full month. Others do not know how much they spend every month in taking the family out to restaurants. Or how much they spend on drinks. How much they spend on recreational activities. How much they spend on groceries. How much they spend on insurance every month. Most people know how much they spend on some of these things, but when you know how much all your expenditures are, then you can develop a monthly budget. Examining these expenses can be eye-opening—even eye-popping.

You might protest that you don't want to know where every single dollar is going or even take the time to find out. I'll respond that if you want to become a successful investor, you have to develop discipline and this is a good place to start. Try it for a month or two. You can carry a pocket notebook with you, and you can put all receipts in a folder or envelope. You might find that $7 you spend every day for lunch adds up to $147/month for an average work-month of 21 days. This might be acceptable to you, but you also might decide to carry your lunch to work once a week. Let's say this saves you $20/month. You might also find that you take the family out to eat at restaurants on the average 6 times a month at an average of $30 per visit. That totals to $180/month. You decide you'll knock that down to 5 restaurant visits a month and save, say, $20/month. That extra magazine you rarely read and that HBO channel you rarely have time to watch could save you another $10 to $15. I know I'm boring some of you with this, but I think you can see that if you know where all your money is going, you have a better idea where money is being wasted or could be saved. This is money that can potentially be put into an investment portfolio. Most mutual funds allow monthly contributions as low as $50/month, some even $25/month.

Even if you are a higher income earner or high-wealth individual and don't worry about a few extra restaurant tabs each month, it is still important to know where your money is being spent. Even high-income earners and people of wealth should budget.

If you have a computer and user-friendly software, fine, but all you need is a tablet and pencil. Get started by writing down all the categories that you spend money on each month. This might look something like the following:

Groceries
————food
————snacks, beverages
————household items

Housing expenses
————mortgage or rent
————property taxes

————home and liability insurance
————emergency repair fund

Automotive
————loan payments
————gas
————repairs
————insurance

Utilities
————electric bill
————telephone
————regular bill
————long distance
————water and sewer
————garbage services

Restaurants
————workday lunches
————family outings
————bar expenses

Medical
————uncovered doctors' and dentists' fees
————prescriptions

Education
————kids' martial arts classes
————kids' swimming lessons
————kids' piano lessons

Recreation
————golf
————athletic club fees
————books and magazines
————cable TV
————movies

Well, you get the idea. Other categories might include clothing allowances or birthday gifts for relatives. You should also have a "miscellaneous" category for those months where unexpected expenses arise—extraordinary car repairs, a new crown for a bum tooth, and so on. Once you know where all the money is going, you will have a much better idea where you can save, and a good idea of what is left over each month. Once you know these things, you can start another category—investment money.

Even if you use this money to pay off debt at 18% or 10% or a 7.5% adjustable mortgage, you are investing in a sure thing. If you allow $1,000 to compound at 18% to the bank, you will owe $2,000 in 4 years, and $4,000 in eight years. (You should know the **rule of 72**. Divide an interest rate into 72 to get the doubling time of the principal. $72/18 = 4$ years for the principal to double in value. An 8% interest rate takes $72/8 = 9$ years to double a principal.) Paying off this debt is equivalent to investing at 18%. Pay off your debt first.

To summarize, budget every month before you start spending your income. Write down the following:

1. Revenue—what you earn, interest income, etc.

2. Expenses—what you spend (as outlined above)

3. Net Income—(Revenue minus Expenses)

Your net income increases if revenue increases or expenses decrease, or both. Your net income is available to increase your assets or to pay down your liabilities. Your net income is the key to wealth creation—and the discretionary funds that can be used to invest and cause your net worth to grow even faster.

We will return to this Income Statement below.

A Plan to Build Wealth

With your budget sheet in hand, develop the habit of recording at periodic intervals (monthly is fine) your personal balance sheet. This balance sheet will have three parts:

1. Assets—what you own (list everything)

2. Liabilities—what you owe (list everything)

3. Net Worth—Assets minus Liabilities

Your list of assets might look like the following:

1. Fair market value of house and household furnishings

2. Fair market value of automobiles

3. Checking and savings accounts

4. Bank CDs and US Savings Bonds

5. Cash value of life insurance

6. Present market value of stocks, bonds and mutual funds

7. Present market value of coins and jewelry

8. After tax value of all retirement accounts

Most people will have other items to add to this list. Find the total value of your list.

Now make a list of all your liabilities—a list of everything you owe. Your list might look like the following:

1. Remaining principal on your first and/or second mortgages

2. Remaining principal on car loans

3. All outstanding credit card balances

4. Any outstanding balances on household purchases

5. Any personal business debt

6. Any outstanding margin balances on brokerage accounts.

Some people may have other debts as well. Include any others and find the total.

Now subtract your total liabilities from your total assets. This is your net worth. The objective of this exercise and of this guide is to increase this number—your net worth.

If you've never performed this exercise, it can be a bit tedious the first time through it. However, if you keep your personal balance sheet up to date, the amount of work involved each month will be rather minimal. This exercise can be eye-opening, too. You might find that your net worth is greater than you would have thought. Or you might find that your net worth is negative. In any case, the drill is necessary and therapeutic.

There are other advantages of going through these exercises. Save these personal income statements and balance sheets and you will have a financial record of your life which you can use as a reference or which can be used to educate children in budgeting and planning. On the back of your income statement record all expenses that are tax deductible. You will have an annual record for the IRS and you will have your taxes half done each year as you refer to your 12 monthly statements. Also as you progress through the year, keep track of major expenses—insurance premiums, property taxes, memberships and dues, vacations—so that you can anticipate these expenditures in the future and plan your cash balances accordingly. Always avoid borrowing if you can.

After you've gone through this exercise, some of you may find that it is advantageous to view net income and net worth on a family basis—i.e., there may be tax benefits in transferring some assets to children or grandchildren. The Uniform Gift to Minors Act allows each parent to give each child up to $10,000 per year without affecting future estate tax exemptions (consult an attorney or tax expert). Children earning interest or dividends are usually taxed at a much lower rate because of their overall lower income. One drawback of transferring assets to children is they will own the assets when they are no longer minors and can sell them and spend the proceeds as they like. On the other hand, by shifting assets out of your direct ownership you may be able to reduce estate taxes upon your death (see chapter on The Investment Nobody Wants).

One last note before closing this section. With all these important and extremely confidential papers, including tax records, you may want to consider a fireproof safe. You can keep other valuables, such as jewelry, coins, even firearms, in a safe as well. You might be surprised how much safe you can buy for a very reasonable price. Remember, too, that this is a one time expense—a good safe will last you a lifetime. I can recommend Liberty Safe Co. Their address and phone number are:

Liberty Safes
1881 E. 7000 S
Salt Lake City, Utah 84121
(801)-942-6565

Call them to find their distributor nearest you.

Make Banking Work for You

Banks are in business to make money. They make money by lending money that you deposit. They also make money by charging you fees. Bankers love two types of people: (1) those that bounce a lot of checks and cannot keep a minimum balance in their checking account, and (2) those that can deposit or borrow millions of dollars at a time. If you are in the first category, you are paying tremendous fees, so the bank really loves you. You need to sit down and start your budget today so those banks will not like you so much.

But even if you do not bounce checks and even if you do maintain a minimum balance in your checking account, you will still encounter plenty of banking fees. Don't assume all banks are the same. Shop around. Go to your yellow pages and call different banks in your area. Ask them about their free checking product or their thrifty "community reinvestment act" checking account. Find out about their minimum balance requirements and their fees for dipping below this amount. Some banks may have much lower minimum balance requirements than others. Also ask about their policy and fees for bounced checks. Some banks might waive fees on the first check you bounce. Ask how much they charge for checks—and whether there are some conditions under which this fee can be waived. Find out how much they charge for safe deposit boxes of different sizes. In this way you can determine which bank would be the most suitable for your needs. You may even find that your bank will negotiate some fees, but don't try this if your accounts are too small.

The next step you may want to take, before opening an account, is to determine, or at least get an opinion, on the soundness of your bank. The size of a bank has nothing to do with its stability. Many smaller or medium-sized banks have much better balance sheets than the major banks. However, throughout the 1990s there has been tremendous consolidation in the banking sector, larger banks swallowing up smaller banks, two medium-sized or even two large banks merging. Every indication in the financial press is that this process will continue. Some of these consolidations bring greater strength and stability, some do not. What is happening is that competition is decreasing, fees are increasing, staff is being cut back and some services are disappearing. These are some reasons it is necessary for you to shop around.

One place you can check the soundness of your bank is Weiss Research, Inc. Their address is:

Weiss Research, Inc.
4176 Burns Road
Palm Beach Gardens, FL 33410
(800)-289-9222

They rate banks on an A to F scale. They will give you a verbal rating for $15, a one page written brief for $25 and an in-depth report of the last 5-years' results for $45. You can also check your local library to see whether they carry Weiss' Ratings Bank Safety Directory. If your library doesn't carry this directory, it might be wise to spend the $15. I recommend that you deal only with banks having a rating of C+ or higher.

Another rating agency is Thomson BankWatch. Their address is:

Thomson BankWatch
61 Broadway, Third Floor
New York, NY 10006
(212)-845-0309

They are the world's largest bank rating service, providing research and analysis on over 1,000 banks in more than 80 countries. Weiss Research is probably more appropriate for the small investor, but if you are connected to the internet you can access Thomson BankWatch at:

www.bankwatch.com

On the subject of bank safety, allow me to digress for a paragraph. Frequently, some financial newsletter writer or other would lead you to believe that the US banking system is on the verge of collapse, for whatever reason. I do not believe this and neither should you. The banking sector goes through cycles, just as every other sector of the economy and all investment classes do. This is an important lesson you should learn from this guide. In the 1970s and early 1980s many large US banks overextended credit to developing countries, primarily south of our border, and ran into difficulties. In the late 1980s many US banks (and Savings and Loans—S&Ls) overextended credit to the commercial real estate sector. In both cases these "crises" were addressed and remedied. In early 2000 the US banking system seems as sound as it's ever been. That is not to say that some other crisis won't arise next month or next year. But should a new crisis arise I have every confidence that it, too, will be addressed and remedied. The banking sector is the backbone of our economy. Too many powerful interests exist to allow the banking system to collapse. Please don't paralyze yourself worrying about these phantom calamities. Newsletter writers conjure up all kinds of disaster scenarios to sell you their products (see chapter on Conspiracies, Gurus and Such).

Of course, some of the most poorly managed banks might collapse even in the best of times—banks are businesses run by human beings with all their foibles. Check out your bank's rating before you open an account.

A Very Conservative Investment

A bank CD is a form of debt security. The bank borrows money from you and pays you interest over a fixed period of time, the maturity of the CD. In recent years bank CDs have not been the place for the best investment returns. Nevertheless, for the more conservative investor this might be a good place to put a portion of your portfolio. Shorter term CDs are also a good place to keep that non-discretionary money that you need for home repairs or other emergencies. The principal is safe and should be covered by FDIC (Federal Deposit Insurance Corporation) as long as your deposit is $100,000 or less. Even this limitation can be skirted by putting one CD in your own name, another in your spouse's name, a third in both names, and so on. Nevertheless it is always best to ask if your CD is covered by FDIC.

Just as you want to shop around for a bank to do your checking and other everyday financial affairs, so you can shop around for the best CD deals. Just because you have a checking account and safe deposit box at one bank doesn't mean you cannot have a CD at another (reasonably rated) bank. It's my experience that banks in a given area sometimes compete to offer the best CD interest rate, at least for one length of maturity. Also, banks often have "specials" that sometimes surprisingly offer substantially better returns compared to their normal rates for the same or similar lengths of maturity.

You also want to find out about early withdrawal penalties. You should not buy a CD with a distant date to maturity if you feel you are going to need that money before the CD matures. Some banks can impose a 3-month or 6-month loss of interest if a CD is redeemed before it matures. On the other hand, many banks offer at least one CD with no or minimal early withdrawal penalties. You will most likely receive less interest on this CD, but if you feel you will redeem early it is better to receive less interest than to receive none at all for a 3-or 6-month period.

My personal preference is not to buy a CD with a maturity of over 2-years, unless the bank is offering a very special deal. The reason is that interest rates can be volatile and nobody knows what they will be 3-, 4-or 5-years down the road. I prefer to take a slightly smaller inter-est rate now in anticipation of much higher interest rates several years in the future. In addition I simply prefer not to tie up my money up for such long periods. You may feel differently.

Summary

A budget is nothing more than a set of goals for your money. You must know where your money is going if you are to maximize your dis-cretionary funds. You are your own company, or your own corporation if you will, and you have a corresponding personal balance sheet. You should be aware of all your assets and liabilities and with your budget make plans to increase your assets and decrease your liabilities, the only way to increase your net worth.

You will most likely need banking services for your day-to-day financial needs. Not all banks are equal—some have lower fees, some have better service, some are rated higher because of their overall financial strength. Shop around to find the best bank to suit your needs.

A bank CD is a conservative investment instrument. There's nothing wrong with having bank CDs as part of your portfolio and, indeed, you should probably keep your non-discretionary money in a CD with short term maturity. When you are in the market for a CD, shop around for the best deals from the best banks.

References

The following are books to help you in planning and goal setting for a better life, the real purpose of this chapter and guide. I list them in the order of my preference.

1. David J. Schwartz, *The Magic of Thinking Big*, Cornerstone Library/Simon and Schuster, New York, NY, 1979.

2. Napoleon Hill, *Think and Grow Rich*, Fawcett Crest, Greenwich, CT, 1963.

3. Rich Pitino with Bill Reynolds, *Success is a Choice*, Broadway Books, New York, NY, 1997.

4. Alan Lakein, *How to Get Control of Your Time and Your Life*, Signet/New American Library, 1973.

5. Maxwell Maltz, *Psycho-Cybernetics*, Pocket Books, New York, NY, 1960.

6. Norman Vincent Peale, *The Power of Positive Thinking*, Fawcet Crest, Greenwich, CT, 1956.

7. Dale Carnegie, *How to Win Friends and Influence People*, Pocket Books, New York, NY, 1964.

Chapter 3

The Investment Nobody Wants

Increasingly, savers and investors will be looking to special life insurance policies as one of the few ways to accumulate money tax deferred.

Jane Bryant Quinn, 1986

This chapter is about life insurance. Even if I could get up on a table in front of you and jump up and down and scream all the while, you still might not believe what I'm going to say about it. This is one of those subjects that most people don't want to hear about, but I dearly urge you to read on.

It's true that everyone should own automobile, liability and property/home insurance. These are usually givens for most rational people, and we treat the premiums as nuisances, just as we do local taxes. When it comes to life insurance, however, even the most-intelligent, best-educated people can come up with lame, irrational excuses for not owning policies or for not owning policies nearly large enough. Most life insurance agents have heard the following comments:

"I can get a much better return on my money elsewhere." (Brave words, indeed, in a roaring bull market.)

"I have a lot of accident insurance. If I die at my age, it'll probably be in an accident."

"I have cheap term insurance with my professional organization. I won't need life insurance when I get older."

"My wife can get a job if I die."

"I don't want my kids to have a lot of money just handed to them."

Yes, there are people who feel this way, but you don't want to be one of them.

Most of us have first hand knowledge of some relatively young person being afflicted with a heart attack, a brain tumor, or some unusual virus. In my own neighborhood just a couple of years ago a 36-year old man was thrown from his bicycle and died of head injuries, leaving behind a wife and three small children. I have no knowledge of his insurance program. Even if a young person were to survive a heart attack or a brain tumor, the chances of getting life insurance after these events is nil. You should buy life insurance at as young an age as possible, when you are your healthiest, and you should buy as much as you can possibly afford at that time. However, if you have neglected to do this, do not let this prevent you from buying life insurance now.

There are many reasons for owning life insurance—providing for a spouse, insuring a child's education, facilitating a smooth business transition, leaving a charitable endowment—but whatever your individual situation one of the most important reasons is that insurance can provide instant liquidity to beneficiaries of your estate. Wills and living trusts can be complicated documents. You better have one or the other—check your state laws. (If you do not have one or the other, stop reading this guide immediately and make suitable arrangements. Don't try to do these yourself—consult an attorney.)

The beneficiary of a life insurance policy can be an individual or individuals, an estate, a trust, or other legal entity such as a corporation or charitable foundation. Life insurance proceeds are paid directly to the beneficiaries of the policy and are free from income taxes. These proceeds, if directed properly, do not have to become part of an estate. These are important points to understand. Life insurance proceeds can provide a cushion during probate which can drag on for months. Making an estate or trust the beneficiary of a life insurance policy can provide instant liquidity to the estate and may prevent the sale of other non-liquid assets at an inappropriate time, in other words, during a down market. This may be the route that has to be followed if minor children are involved. Such proceeds could also keep a family business intact in the face of stiff estate taxes.

All estates over $675,000 must pay estate taxes (this exclusion is scheduled to increase to $1 million by 2006). However, a surviving spouse does not have to pay estate taxes on property held jointly because of the so-called martial deduction. But when the second spouse passes on, all such property will now be included in the remaining estate. A husband and wife can set up their estates (and wills) in such a way that the first to die may leave $675,000 to children or other beneficiaries. This not only reduces the estate value of the second spouse, but this estate also receives the $675,000 exclusion. In this way their beneficiaries can receive a total of $1.35 million free of estate taxes.

There also exist "second-to-die" life insurance policies. These policies are based on the lives of two people, usually husband and wife. The death benefit of the policy is paid only when the second of these two individuals passes away. These policies have several attractive features. First, for the same amount of insurance they typically have substantially reduced premiums compared to an individual policy. Second, they can sometimes be issued even when one of the two insured might not be able to obtain life insurance alone. Third, they can usually be structured to be paid-up after a fixed number of years. Finally, these policies are especially convenient for charitable giving or for placing in a trust for the express purpose of paying estate taxes (always consult competent professionals before setting up special situations).

Because life insurance provides for loved ones and adds liquidity to an estate, it is one of the basic building blocks or cornerstones to any investment program. No matter what other investment instruments you own, no matter whether you are wealthy or not-so-wealthy, if you do not have a solid life insurance program, you do not have a well-rounded, complete investment portfolio. In the remainder of this chapter I will discuss what constitutes a solid life insurance program and how to get into one.

The Company

Picking the right insurance company can be a major headache. There are no more than about ten companies in the United States that I would recommend dealing with. All these companies are rated A or A+ by Weiss Research, Inc., located in Palm Beach Gardens, Florida. Weiss rates over 1600 insurance companies on a scale of A+ to F with the latter rating meaning that the company has failed and is probably under the auspices of the state insurance commissioner's office. Only 3.4% of the companies have a rating of A or A+. Weiss also lists a number of very small companies with a U rating—avoid these. You can reach Weiss Research at (800)-289-9222. They will give you a verbal credit rating on a company for $15, a one page written brief for $25 and an 18-page report with portfolio breakdown and the last 5-year's results for $45. To save money, you can check your local public library to see whether they carry Weiss' Ratings Insurance Safety Directory.

Recently the Government Accounting Office concluded that Weiss' insurance company ratings are superior to the other five rating companies. A.M. Best Company gave Mutual Benefit its highest rating at the same time that Weiss Research was issuing warning signs. Speak consolingly if you know any policyholders of Mutual Benefit. A couple of years back, Mutual Benefit was paying about 55¢ on the dollar to people who were opting out of its policies and raising premiums to double or more to people who wanted to keep the insurance in force. Martin Weiss' *Safe Money Report* recommended opting out.

In short, spend the $15 if you can't get the information from the library. Only buy insurance from a company that is rated A or A+, preferably A+, by Weiss Research.

The Agent

You narrowed down the companies, now you need an agent. Agents are one of the biggest reasons life insurance has a bad name. In many cases agents are too young and too ill-prepared to represent their product. The agent may be either overly aggressive or under severe pressure from the company to prove himself. Six months down the road he may be representing another company or working in another profession. This leads to discontinuity in your program, perhaps resulting in improper attention being paid to your account. The blame for such problems lies ultimately with the insurance companies in their never-ending exploitation of young salespeople.

Nevertheless, in every community there are the experienced, knowledgeable insurance agents working with Weiss rated A+ companies. These agents know their craft well. Keep passing until you find such a person—he can bring you guidance and understanding, confidence and solace. He will be familiar with the creative applications of life insurance (note that I did not say "creative life insurance"). He will be on friendly terms with other competent professionals with whom you may have to deal (i.e., attorneys, accountants, tax advisors, etc.). Most importantly he will treat you like a long-term customer, not a quick sale.

It is true that young agents can grow with their clients, but let others grow with theirs. You seek out the experienced pro.

The policy

I'm sorry—you're going to hate me on this one. The type of policy you should own is genuine **whole life** or as much whole life as you can comfortably afford. If you simply cannot afford to cover all your insurance needs with whole life, then cover the remainder in term-insurance that has the option of later allowing you to convert to whole life.

Financial planners who are selling a variety of products or financial writers who are trying to be ever-so-clever will tell you to buy term insurance only and put the money you saved by not buying whole life into stocks or mutual funds. This argument sounds rational and alluring. After all, why not save money? Why not get the big return in the stock market with the difference? At the sake of sounding brash, allow me to say that these advisors and their thinking are dead wrong. Period. Why? Because life insurance should be one of the cornerstones of your investment portfolio. It is there to provide stability to the portfolio. It is there to provide for loved ones and to give instant liquidity to your estate. It should without question be one of the investment classes into which you diversify.

But people will protest: can't I accomplish all this with term insurance? No, you cannot. First of all, term insurance builds no wealth. Therefore, it cannot represent an investment class. Term insurance lasts for a specified period of time, the term, typically one year, when it is renewed. Some companies and professional organizations will guarantee a premium for a given number of years, but, in general, term insurance becomes more expensive as a person ages. In fact, by the time a person approaches 60 years of age and beyond, the cost of term insurance increases exponentially (for the less mathematically inclined, exponential means *real steep*). It can become prohibitively expensive. The other problem with term insurance is that most companies do not even offer it to persons past 70 years of age, or shortly thereafter. If you want life insurance into your retirement years and beyond, and I have argued that you should want this, then term is not for you. As whole investors we should get used to the idea that we will carry at least part of our whole life insurance program with us to the grave. We may not like thinking about these things, but we should plan for it.

By all means, avoid Universal Life like the plague. It is an example of "creative life insurance" (not a creative application of life insurance). Universal Life is nothing more than term insurance plus a side investment vehicle. The side investment is supposed to grow so fast as to offset the ever-increasing cost of the term insurance at older ages. Universal Life was developed in the late 1970s when inflation rates were in the high teens and money market funds were paying 16-17% returns (yes, I remember those days). A side investment paying 17% per annum would, indeed, be a powerful companion to a term policy, but many of you know that interest rates fell through most of the 1980s and reached a low of around 3% in the 1993-94 period. Even as I write this guide, money market rates are barely over 5%. It can be argued that "creative" policies such as Universal Life is what caused some insurance companies considerable financial pain in the late 1980s and early 1990s. Trying to maintain a high return on these investment side-instruments, the companies gambled on riskier and riskier investments such as junk bonds and questionable real estate.

Variable life insurance is another attempt to jazz up a policy. Variable life can be combined with either universal or whole life. Basically, variable life is like having a mutual fund attached to your life insurance policy. Your investment funds or cash value can then be switched (varied) from say a money market fund to a bond fund to a stock fund. The problem I have with variable life is that it represents a distinct mixing of investment classes. Let's face it, during the 1990s-2000 equity bull market most people who bought variable life chose to be in a stock fund. But the life insurance portion of your portfolio is supposed to be one of the most stable, conservative areas of your diversified investments. Always keep in mind the reasons you want life insurance as one of your investment classes: loved ones, estate liquidity. Do you really want to expose this portion of your portfolio to the vagaries of a much riskier investment class? When you have all your insurance needs met with solid no-frills whole life, then fine—take a flier with variable whole life. But then and only then.

You Own It

You found a great company (rated A or A+ by Weiss Research), you found a fantastic, experienced agent, and you bought a solid whole life policy. Now you should know a few important things about your policy. First, *you own the policy*, the company does not own it. In fact, if your policy is with a mutual insurance company, as opposed to a stock-owned company, you have become part owner of the company. I highly recommend a mutual insurance company over a stock-owned insurance company, because in a mutual company the policy owners come first whereas in a stock-owned company (reality check, as Dan Rather would say) the shareholders come first. The owners of a company make the decisions affecting the company. It only makes sense that if push comes to shove in a stock-owned company, the owners are going to vote in their own self-interest, not the policyholders'. Go with a mutual insurance company.

The cash value that builds up in a policy (this should be set up to accumulate tax-deferred) is *your* money, not the company's money. The yearly dividend (this, too, should be set up to accumulate tax-deferred) is also *your* money. It is amazing how many people do not realize that they own their life insurance policies, or do not realize that the cash value and dividend are their money. I don't know—maybe most companies are afraid that if people truly understood these concepts they would take their money out of their policies and invest it in the stock market. However, you as a whole investor—suitably diversified and disciplined in money management—will not do that. Leave the money in the policy to accumulate tax-deferred. Whole life insurance policies are one of the great tax shelters still available to the average person.

What annoys most people about whole life insurance is that it usually takes from five to ten years or longer, depending upon the policy and company, to break even. In other words, it takes this amount of time to build your cash value equal to the amount you've paid in. For sake of argument, let's say this sequence takes eight years. Think about it—in eight years time you now have available all the money that you invested in the policy, plus you've had eight years of insurance protection. It's almost like getting the insurance for free. This isn't entirely true, because there is the lost opportunity time during which you might have received interest, for example. On the other hand, any money you would have spent on term insurance during that time, along with its opportunity time, is definitely lost.

A point I have to make about life insurance is that you have to pay for the insurance protection one way or another. You do not get something for nothing. Pay me now or pay me later as the advertisement used to say. In the case of whole life you pay up front by losing the investment potential of the premiums paid during those early years.

Continuing with the example above in which you break even after eight years, something wonderful happens during the ninth year and beyond. You still have the life insurance in place along with the cash value, but now for every additional dollar you pay in premium, you receive a very reasonable return. In fact, I know of policies where in the fifteenth year or so for every dollar of premium paid that year a return of $2.00 or more is returned in cash value. Believe me, doubling your money in a year in most investments is very difficult to do. But wait a minute, you say. Surely I'm pulling the wool over your eyes. No, honest. With a good company and with your policy set up correctly (dividends should be used to purchase paid-up additions) you can double or even triple your yearly premium if you stick with the program long enough. But you do have to pay for the insurance sometime, those first years that you are breaking even.

Your whole life insurance policy can also turn into a wonderful supplemental retirement program. Remember: all that cash value has been accumulating tax-deferred and it's your money. But at age 62, or 65 or 67 or at whatever age you want, you can change the way the dividend on that cash value is treated. You can ask your agent to keep your paid-up insurance in place but change the dividend option so that the dividend is now paid directly to you. I believe most insurance companies can set this up to be paid annually, semi-annually, quarterly or monthly. You pay no taxes until you receive an amount equal to the total premiums you paid in over the years (consult your tax advisor). You may even find that your circumstances have changed and you don't need as much liquidity in your estate as you had assumed (be careful here). In that case you can cash in part or even all the insurance and use part or all of the cash value to set up an annuity. A good agent should be able to suggest other options as well.

Attempting to use a Universal Life policy as a retirement vehicle can be a lot more tricky. Note there is no paid-up insurance in these policies so your options are much more limited. If you start taking the dividend out of the policy, since the term insurance is now becoming so costly, you may quickly eat into the cash value and destroy the policy. Of course, you can always cancel the insurance policy and use the cash value to set up an annuity.

Summary

In this chapter I've tried to convince you that whole life insurance has a definite place as one of the investment classes in your diversified portfolio. It need not be one of the major portions of your portfolio. Though I didn't plan it this way originally, because of the compounding of my cash value, I am finding that life insurance is becoming one of my major holdings. Am I sad about this? Not at all. I plan to continue paying premiums and letting that cash value build.

I've also tried to convince you that you have to get over this hurdle of worrying about paying for the insurance in those early years, those years when you are just breaking even. There's no free lunch. In whole life policies you pay for the insurance up front, just as in a mortgage you pay most of the interest charges up front.

Start looking for that veteran agent who works for one of the top rated companies. Then set yourself up with a solid whole life program. Have the discipline to stick with it. You won't be sorry.

References

I've never found a book or other reference that I really liked on life insurance, outside of company specific material. Most give short shift to whole life insurance and extol the virtues of term and Universal Life. They are wrong—dead wrong. I give a reference on estate planning, which may be updated by now.

1. Robert A. Esperti and Renno L. Peterson, *The Handbook of Estate Planning*, McGraw-Hill, New York, 1991.

A book on related topics, including estate planning is:

2. Terry Coxon, *Keep What You Earn*, Times Business/Randon House, New York, 1996.

Chapter 4

So You Want to Own A Company?

Bulls get rich and bears get rich, but pigs get slaughtered.

A well-known Wall Street saying

One of those great capitalist ideas is stock shares in a company allowing individuals to become part owners of the company. Though it is not absolutely necessary to have a brokerage account in order to own stocks (some companies permit direct purchases of stock through a *d*ividend *re-i*nvestment *p*lan or DRIP), it is customary and convenient to do so. Whenever you buy or sell stock, you receive or surrender a stock certificate that contains information about the company and the number of shares you purchased. The certificate can be in your name or the brokerage firm's name (referred to as the street name) depending upon whether you want the certificate in your possession or you want the brokerage house to store it for you. Nowadays most certificates are kept in safekeeping by brokerage houses.

Brokerage firms facilitate the purchase and sale of stock shares as well as perform other services for their clients. They receive a commission each time a purchase or sale is made. You should be aware that there are full service (full commission) brokerage firms and discount brokerage firms. Full commission firms provide a variety of services for their clients, including advice on stock selection, analysts' reports and so on. Discount firms typically provide only the basic services of buying and selling shares, giving basic stock quotes and holding stocks in street name. Many firms also provide electronic trading over a personal computer and the commissions on these trades can be deeply discounted. Commissions may vary depending on the price of the stock and the number of shares transacted.

How much difference is there among full, discount and deeply discounted commissions? In a word: substantial. A discount commission may be a half to a third or less of a full commission. A deeply discounted commission may be a half to one third of a discount commission. Am I suggesting you do your stock trading electronically? Yes, if you own a personal computer with Internet connection. If you do not own a personal computer with Internet connection, then use a discount broker. The less money you waste on commissions, the more money you will have to put to work for your portfolio. I'm certain there are many people who have wonderful relationships with their full commission brokers and have made significant returns using their services. However, the aim of this guide is to develop the whole investor who will not need these hand-holding services. Frequently the stock recommendations from these brokers are no better than those you could develop from your own research (e.g., from reading *Investor's Business Daily*, *Barron's*, etc., for starters). Sometimes they are much worse. Sometimes you may get a call from your full commission broker pushing a stock that a much larger client is trying to unload.

The largest discount broker is Charles Schwab & Company, based in San Francisco, but with offices throughout the country. I've been a client for many years, long before I began studying investing seriously. I can highly recommend them. They have an excellent web page for traders who want to do all their trading electronically. The commissions on most trades are $29.95, though they have lowered commissions for active traders and will probably be forced to lower commissions across the board in the future. I've been plugged in the past several years, and I must confess have never enjoyed trading stocks more. On a hundred-share trade, I'm only out a little over a quarter point on either side of the trade. The same trade with a full commission broker could end up costing me one to two points on either side of the trade. The advice from a full commission broker better be awfully good to make up that difference.

The addresses and telephone numbers for several discount brokers, including Charles Schwab, follow:

Charles Schwab & Company
The Schwab Building
101 Montgomery Street
San Francisco, CA 94104-9979
(800)-435-4000
www.schwab.com

E*Trade Securities, Inc
Four Embarcadero Place
2400 Geng Road
Palo Alto, CA 94303
(800)-786-2573
www.etrade.com

Fidelity Investments
82 Devonshire Street
Boston, MA 02109
(800)-544-9697
www.fidelity.com

DLJ Direct
Harborside Financial Center
501 Plaza II
Jersey City, NJ 07311
(800)-825.5723
www.DLJdirect.com

I could include in this chapter a lot of trivia about stocks and the stock market such as: **blue chips** are the largest, most consistently profitable companies, the term coming from the most valuable chip in poker. And the US stock markets has traded in **eighths** (now sixteenths—and a change to decimals is coming soon) because of a carry over from the old octagonal Spanish and Spanish-American dollars which could be cut into pieces of eight. You are likely to forget most of this information anyway, and though it is interesting it really won't help your trading. More of this kind of information is included in some of the references at the end of the chapter.

More important concepts you should not forget include the P-E Ratio of a stock, or its **P/E**, which is the price of a stock divided by its annual earnings per share. Note that a stock's P/E can be large if either the price is very high or the earnings are small, or both. Investors are willing to buy high P/E stocks if the companies are growing rapidly and earnings are expected to rise significantly in the future. More typical P/Es historically are in the low to mid-teens, although in times of a bear market the average P/E for the Standard and Poors 500 could be in the single digits, while in the euphoria of a bull market this average P/E could rise into the high 20s or even into the 30s. The P/Es of stocks with no or nil earnings and those with losses are listed in the stock tables with three dots: ... .

It is unwise to base your trading solely on a stock's P/E. As mentioned above, some of the fastest growing companies sport high P/Es. On the other hand, stocks with low P/Es are not always a bargain. You should, however, always be aware of a stock's P/E relative to its market sector. If the general P/E for technology stocks is 30 to 40 and you are contemplating purchasing a tech stock with a P/E of 100, you now know that it is a "high flyer" and could likely come crashing back down to earth.

Another concept you should be familiar with is a stock's **yield**. This is the annual dividend divided by the stock price. This number is usually multiplied by a hundred to get a percentage yield. Certain sectors such as utilities and financial stocks tend to have higher yields. Some of the fastest growing companies pay no dividends, plowing their earnings instead into research and development, so consequently their yield is zero. Some investors buy high yielding stocks for the return plus a small expected appreciation in stock price. Other investors buy stocks with no dividends on the expectation of significant appreciation in stock price.

Another subject you should be aware of is **stock splits**. Shareholders can approve a stock split of some multiple so that the number of outstanding shares changes by that multiple. The price of the stock changes accordingly. If a $50 stock with 10 million shares outstanding undergoes a 2 for 1 stock split, the 20 million new shares will each be worth $25. Stocks can be split in any multiples. Splits of 2 for 1, 3 for 1 and 3 for 2 are common. The process of splitting a stock does not in itself enhance the share value, but a stock often appreciates soon after the split. This can be attributed to the stock now being affordable to more investors, who then pile in. It is not clear that a stock split is always good for the long-term prospects of a company, however. Some pundits argue that stock splitting is designed to enable insiders to "distribute" their high priced shares to the often gullible and clueless public. Reverse splits are also possible. If a $2 stock with 50 million shares outstanding is reverse split 1 for 5, then the 10 million shares of the new stock are worth $10.

More of this kind of information is available in the references as well. As new concepts arise, I will define them as needed. Since this is a "how to" book, in the next sections of this chapter I will concentrate on two distinctively different techniques for stock selection. Both techniques work. As you do further reading you will find out about other techniques for stock selection that work also. The trick again as in other facets of investing is discipline. Find a technique that is compatible with your temperament and implement it.

The Ted Warren Stock Picking Method

I was fortunate, some twenty years ago, that my brother happened to stumble upon Ted Warren's, *How to Make the Stock Market Make Money for You*, copyrighted in 1966. Even though neither of us had much money twenty years ago, we immediately and almost literally devoured the book. We have since used the techniques described therein with convincing success. This title had been out of print for a significant number of years, but my understanding is that the Ken Roberts

Company obtained the copyright and has reissued the book under the Four Star Books label. I will give you the gist of the method in the following paragraphs, but if this technique suits your temperament you should obtain a complete copy and thoroughly read it, then reread it. The address is:

Four Star Books
128 Southwest I Street
Grants Pass, OR 97526
(800)-350-2350

Note that the examples in Mr. Warren's book date from the pre-1966 period. Some of the companies discussed there have either merged or no longer exist. You should not concern yourself about this, however, because I will show below that his ideas are still valid into the year 2000.

The basic concept behind the Ted Warren method (this concept is not unique to Mr. Warren) is that all stocks undergo periods of accumulation and distribution. Mr. Warren was a cynic and severe critic of Wall Street. He suggested that the insiders and smart money (the strong hands) bought stocks during the accumulation phase, when the stock was selling at bargain prices, and that these people sold to the naive public (weak hands) after the price had already risen by significant amounts. Once most of the stock was in the public's hands there were only the greater fools left to buy so eventually the stock price would fall of its own weight and the process would begin all over again. Similar theories are prevalent in 2000 because of the heights reached by many stocks. Mr. Warren, being the cynic he was, further suggested that all public pronouncements from Wall Street on a given company were devised to achieve this very effect.

The key to the method, according to Mr. Warren, is that these periods of accumulation and distribution can be determined from **long term charts** of the stock price. You don't have to be the cynic Mr.

Warren was to make the method work for you, as I will show with a few examples. The charts shown in this guide were obtained using SuperCharts 4.0 software distributed by Omega Research. The data used is obtained from Omega Research and Dial Data on CD disk and from Dial Data, an on-line data provider, via modem download. Their addresses are:

Omega Research	Dial Data
9200 Sunset Drive	56 Pine Street
Miami, FL 33173-3266	New York, NY 10005
(800)-422-8587	(800)-275-5544
www.omegaresearch.com	www.tdc.com/ddhp.html

The first example, shown in Figure 4-1 is the monthly price chart of a stock that people either adore or hate, Micron Technology, symbol MU on the NYSE. It is a classic example of what Mr. Warren talks about in his book. There was a multi-year period from the mid-1980s through 1993 when the stock provided little excitement to investors. Mr. Warren's theory would suggest that by the start of 1993 most of the shares, if not all, were held by insiders and the smart money (professional investors), or in his terminology by strong hands. The first real excitement this stock offers occurs in the latter half of 1993. This could be looked upon as a test to see whether there was any buying power for the stock. Notice the dip that occurs after this initial rally. This price decline probably once again puts most or all of the stock in strong hands. This dip or "cup-shaped" structure in the price chart will be important in the second stock selection method discussed later in the chapter.

Once the initial test is accomplished and the stock is again in strong hands the stock goes through a tremendous price rise from early 1994 through mid-1995. During this time the public hears all kinds of exiting news about the company and is only too willing to purchase shares from the strong hands. Finally, after the last burst of euphoria, most of the stock will be in the public's hands. By this time all the good news about the company is out, and the public which is powerless itself to make pronouncements on the company must now trade it among themselves. The stock falls of its own weight. The next question to be answered is whether, by the time the stock had fallen from over 90 to around 18, it is again in strong hands. It is unlikely, even though the stock rallied from this low. These rallies are more likely incentives for the public to sell its remaining shares. An investor who bought at 90 and held through 18 probably looks at 36 as an opportunity to salvage something. Accumulation periods typically take a couple of years, in some cases much longer. Not until the technology rally of the late 1999, early 2000 period has Micron Technology made it back to its old highs.

One question that should be asked here, especially if you ever hear anything about the "efficient market theory" (not discussed in this guide—the author doesn't believe in it), is: can a company whose stock is priced at 10 in the beginning of 1994 really have increased its value by 9 times just a year-and-a-half later (and approximately 18 times from its mid 1992 level)? How efficient could the market possibly have been in this example? The market capitalization of a company (the share price times the number of shares outstanding) should be some reasonable multiple of its real worth. What is the fair share price for Micron Technology? Is it 10, 90, 18 or 60? The "market" doesn't seem to know. Many authors will tell you that the market is always right, yet if you held Micron Technology from 90 to 18 you might be inclined to think differently.

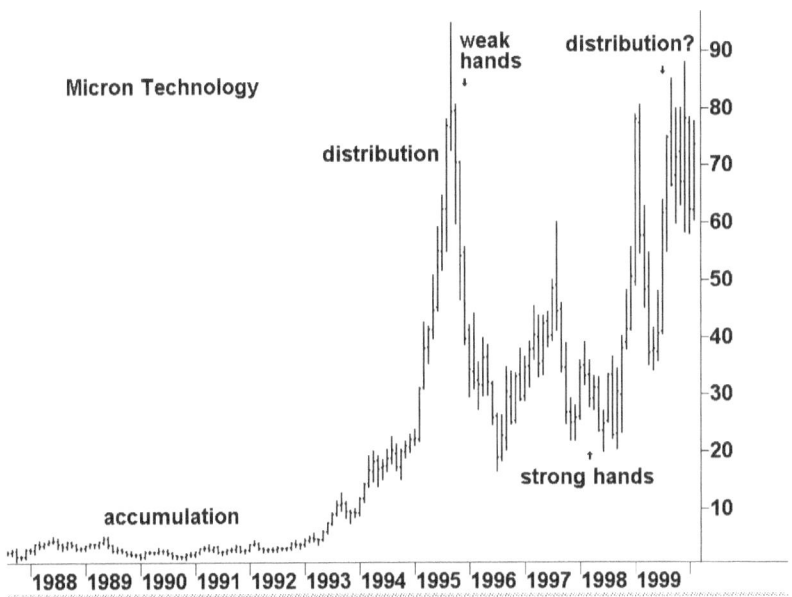

Fig. 4-1

The important lesson to be gleaned from this example, however, even if you're not certain you like Mr. Warren's method, is that you should be aware of the long-term price history of a stock. Anyone in 1995 who had a long-term price chart of Micron Technology could see that at 90 (or for that matter at 60) the stock was expensive by historical standards. On the other hand, anyone in 1998 who knew the long-term price history of Micron Technology could see that the stock at 20 was approaching price support and was relatively inexpensive.

For a second illustration of this method, I use a monthly price chart (Figure 4-2) of Computer Sciences Corporation (CSC—NYSE). I give you this example because there are two distinct periods of accumulation at two distinct price levels. A mild distribution of this stock occurs throughout 1986-87, culminating in the crash of October 1987. A new accumulation period extends from 1987 through 1991 with a dip or cup structure completing in 1991. From there the stock increases in value by approximately four times. A second accumulation period takes place starting in late 1995 and extends into 1997 where we see another dip (cup). The stock goes on to triple in price from the low of that dip. As we enter the year 2000 is this stock undergoing distribution? It's still a little early to tell, but the situation is suspicious. What we can say is that the stock is expensive by historical standards. This does not appear to be the best time to buy into CSC.

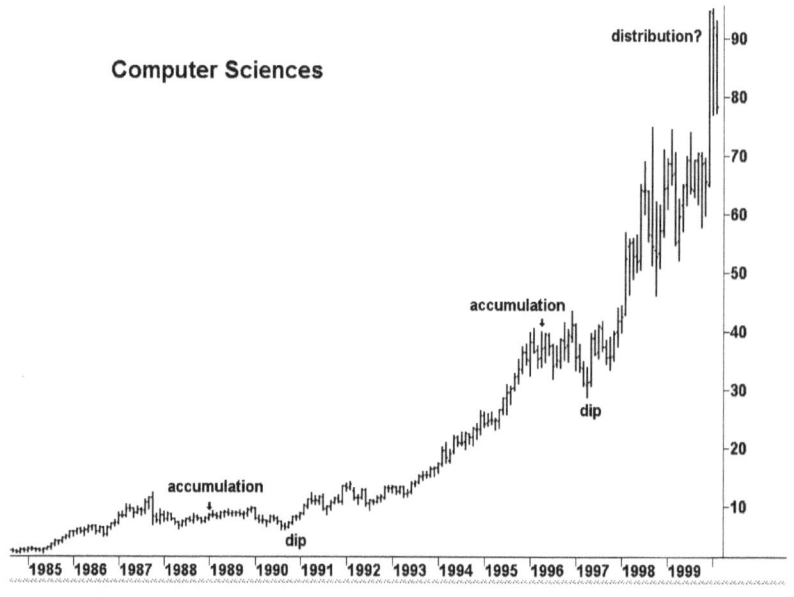

Fig. 4-2

To profit from this method, the whole investor determines from long-term charts when periods of accumulation are taking place. The investor buys along with the insiders and holds his shares for the eventual large move up. This method is not very exciting in the short term. It can take years before a given stock makes its big move. The advantage is that you can accumulate a large number of shares at a very inexpensive price. If you apply this method, you might make a larger allowance for acceptable loss because you will be accumulating shares at various prices within a small range, but you may have to withstand the final dip before the big move. You can make this method more exciting by waiting for the dip following the accumulation period, then buy as the stock recovers past the highest price before the dip occurred. You can determine this price by drawing a horizontal line across the highest price before the dip. This line should form the top of the cup. The advantage of using this modification of Ted Warren's method is that you don't have to hold the shares as long before the up move. The disadvantage is that you will get fewer shares for the same money at this higher level.

A few comments before I move on to the second method of stock selection. First, the number of stocks for which you can spot accumulation periods is much smaller in 2000 than it was in the 1980s or even in the early 1990s. This is saying something about the stock markets in general, namely that many more stocks are expensive today. Second, another way to spot distribution is to note the direction of trading during a given day. If the market (or stock) you are observing moves up early in the day, but cannot hold that level and perhaps retraces its gain or even loses ground by day's end, then you can feel confident that some distribution has occurred. One day of such trading may not be that telling, but if this action occurs on a number of days (or weeks), then the market (or stock) may be in for a tumble.

Finally, you do not have to own a computer and buy charting software in order to follow Mr. Warren's method. Long term stock charts are available for purchase. One such compilation is *The Stock Picture*, published six times a year by M.C. Horsey & Company. In fact, if you are new to the stock market, I recommend you get a copy just to acquaint yourself with the price histories of various stocks. A single issue is $35, a one year subscription $140. The address is:

M.C. Horsey & Company, Inc.
Salisbury, MD 21801
(410)-742-3700

The William J. O'Neil Stock Picking Method

William J. O'Neil is a stock market legend, having even been featured in the national best-selling book *Market Wizards* by Jack D. Schwager (more must reading: see reference at the end of this chapter). If Mr. Ted Warren is a cynic and critic of Wall Street, then Mr. O'Neil must be described as an unbridled optimist of Wall Street and the American economic system. In 1964 he formed William O'Neil and Co., today one of the leading securities research firms in the country, dealing in detailed computerized stock market and securities data. In 1983 he started *Investor's Daily*, now called *Investor's Business Daily (IBD)*, which every business day for the price of a subscription gives you substantial quantities of information from this data base (see Chapter 1 for address and telephone number). *IBD* even offers a free two-week trial subscription that includes an audio tape on how to read and use the newspaper. I think all investors owe it to themselves at least to try the free two-week subscription.

Mr. O'Neil has detailed his stock picking method in the book *How to Make Money in Stocks*. Just as the title gets right to the point, so is the text clear and specific. The book has been included as an incentive with a yearly subscription to *IBD*, but in any case it is now available in soft cover and easily affordable. In the next few paragraphs I will outline Mr. O'Neil's method known as the C-A-N S-L-I-M system, which sounds a little like a new diet plan but which can fatten your pocketbook. This system has been discussed in other publications, as well, including *Technical Analysis of Stocks & Commodities* magazine (see references at end of chapter 10), but if the method suits your temperament I recommend rather than getting a brief outline that you buy the book, read it, study it, underline and highlight. Between Mr. Warren's and Mr. O'Neil's books you will get an excellent overview of not only the way the stock market works but a better feeling for financial markets in general.

Though one element of Mr. Warren's and Mr. O'Neil's method is similar (I mentioned the cup formation above) this aspect, though important, is not crucial to Mr. O'Neil's method. It is difficult to summarize this method in one or two sentences, but the following comes close: (1) Determine what patterns caused successful stocks in the past to surge in price—this is summarized in the C-A-N S-L-I-M system; (2) in using Mr. O'Neil's method look for the best performing companies in the best performing sectors of the market and do not hesitate to buy a stock that is reaching new highs.

Though I cannot do the C-A-N S-L-I-M system justice in this brief discussion, the general outline follows:

C stands for *Current Quarterly Earnings Per Share.* Stocks should show a major percentage increase in the current quarterly earnings per share when compared to the prior year's same quarter. Mr. O'Neil's research showed that nearly all companies with big upward movements in stock price had accelerated quarterly earnings increases some time in the previous ten quarters.

A stands for *Annual Earnings Increases.* Each year's annual earnings per share for the last five years should show an increase over the prior year's earnings. An exception might occur if after earnings are down one year the following year's earnings recover into new high ground. Mr. O'Neil suggests accepting nothing less than stocks with annual growth rates of between 15 to 50%.

N stands for *New Products, New Management, New Highs.* Mr. O'Neil advises that it takes something new to produce a huge advance in the stock price. Also any New Event in the company's industry could be important, such as new technology, industry-wide shortages or price increases.

S stands for Shares of Common Stock Outstanding. Mr. O'Neil suggests that the law of supply and demand is as true for stocks as for anything else. He suggests that stocks with smaller number of shares outstanding can be pushed up in price more quickly because of the limited supply available.

L stands for Leader or Laggard. Mr. O'Neil recommends investing in stocks that are leaders in one of the leading sectors of the market and to avoid laggards even if they are a laggard in a leading sector. His newspaper, IBD, lists a Relative Price Strength using a scale from 1 to 99 for all stocks. The relative price strength compares a stock's price performance against the price action of all other stocks in the tables. Mr. O'Neil advises against investing in any stock whose relative price strength is below 70, and that the best performing stocks for a coming year have been shown to have a relative price strength of 87 or higher.

I stands for Institutional Sponsorship. This means the stock should be owned by at least a few mutual funds, insurance companies, corporate pension funds, hedge funds and so forth. Institutions can create huge demand for a given supply of stock. It is also true, however, that a stock can be "overowned" by institutions.

M stands for Market Direction. Mr. O'Neil argues even if all the other factors in the C-A-N S-L-I-M system are in your favor that three out of four stocks will slump in a general market decline. He advises the best way to determine the direction of the market is to follow and understand every day what the general market averages are doing.

Let me first say that Mr. O'Neil's method works, and works very well, if you are disciplined enough to follow it. Indeed, though the general market has been decidedly up in recent years, I would say that of the various factors in the C-A-N S-L-I-M system determining the overall market direction may be the most difficult. Clearly this stock picking method contrasts with Mr. Warren's, which is basically a buy low during an accumulation phase, sell high during a distribution phase method. Mr. O'Neil's system is a buy high, sell much higher method. The holding period for a stock under Mr. O'Neil's method would be generally much shorter than under Mr. Warren's method.

There are, however, some similarities in the methods. Mr. Warren suggests a stock rises in price because of hype from the company; Mr. O'Neil advises buying when something new happens with the company (i.e., when there's good news—assuming his other factors fall into line). Mr. Warren's method certainly is more valid when the number of shares of a company are smaller in number, because it is then easier for the insiders to accumulate (and distribute) a higher percentage of the stock; Mr. O'Neil points out that stock prices can be pushed higher in value when there is a limited supply. Also from a charting standpoint the two methods have one aspect in common and that is the cup formation mentioned above. Mr. O'Neil recommends buying stocks whose C-A-N S-L-I-M factors have been satisfied and whose price actions have undergone what he refers to as a "cup with handle" formation. As an example, I refer you to Figure 4-3, which shows a weekly chart of Oracle Corporation. There from about March through July 1999 is a fairly well-defined cup with the handle of the cup extending out through September. The stock price then more than tripled over the next few months. In Mr. O'Neil's book you will find many examples of this formation preceding large price moves.

While Mr. O'Neil is eager to follow the newer more exciting companies, Mr. Warren probably never would have looked at a companies like Micron Technology, Computer Sciences Corporation or Oracle Corporation in the first place. He would have preferred older, proven companies that had fallen on hard times, where long periods of unexciting price action proved that accumulation was taking place.

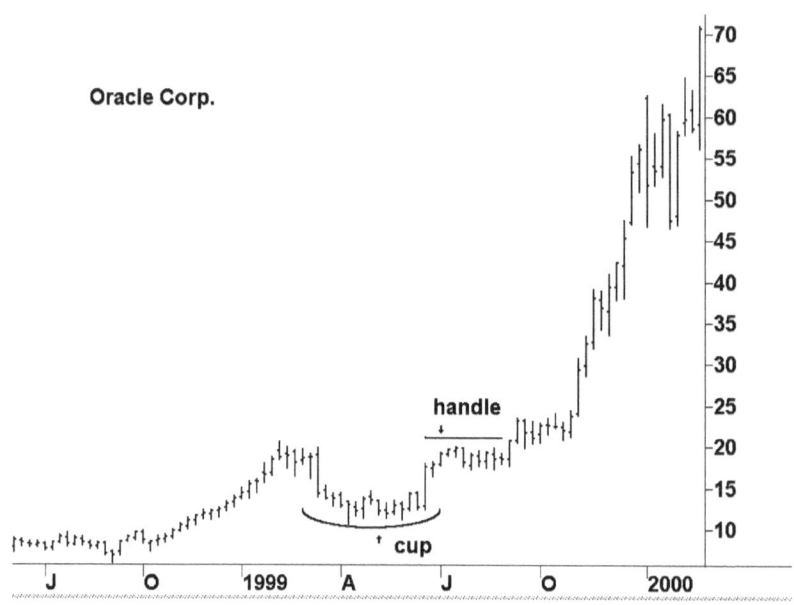

Fig. 4-3

The stock market in 2000

According to various market gurus, the year 2000 bull market in stocks extends from 1977, 1982, 1987 (after the crash), or 1990. Regardless of the date you choose, even the most stubborn bear would have to admit that this period has represented a great opportunity in stock ownership. Many of the greatest fortunes in the history of the world have been made during this time. Will the Great Bull Market in stocks continue, take a breather, or give up the ghost and turn into a great market decline? Naturally, everybody wants the answer to that question, and nearly everybody has his or her own opinion. Since this bull market is long in the tooth by any standard, I feel it my duty in the next few paragraphs to give you some opposing views.

The stock market, as usually thought of in terms of the Dow Jones Industrial Average (Dow 30, or Dow), the Standard and Poors 500 Index (S&P 500), and the Nasdaq composite index has risen dramatically, especially since 1982. However, there are stocks, some included in these averages, others not included, that have done even better and, of course, those that have performed much more poorly. When we hear about the market averages or market indices we get a general feeling for the overall condition of the stock market. We have much less knowledge of any individual stock in these indices, even less so for those stocks not in the averages. So when commentators or financial pundits talk about how if only you would have put x-amount of dollars in Dow stocks on May 26, 1896, the day the Dow average was introduced, then today your portfolio would be worth a kazillion dollars, you really have to take such talk with a grain of salt. Though today it is possible to own shares of mutual funds that exactly mimic the market indices, for individual stock investors this procedure is not practical nor is it clear that it would always be beneficial. Of the original twelve Dow stocks only General Electric is still in the Dow. Many of the other companies of that time have ceased to exist. Just keep in mind that as a stock investor it is individual stocks that you are investing in. Also, because investors are human and occasionally desire to enjoy the fruits of their investments, they might from time to time want to buy a new house or that new Mercedes with their profits or even send a child to Princeton or Harvard. Thus it would be the rare individual who would leave all that money in the Dow stocks since 1886 (such an investor also would have to have an extraordinary long life) or even since 1986.

In this and the following paragraphs I will give some of the pros and cons concerning the continuation of the current Great Bull Market. I'll start off with some of the pros. First, and perhaps foremost, since the late 1980s and early 1990s communism as we knew it has largely disappeared from the planet. Yes, Castro is still alive and the mainland Chinese are still officially communists, but even the mainland Chinese are allowing extensive capitalist expansion. Eastern Europe and the former Soviet Union are now espousing capitalist economies. This has had a number of consequences, most of them positive for our stock market. Our defense budget, as a percentage of GNP, has declined. American companies have been able to penetrate formerly forbidden markets. Literally a couple of billion more consumers for US products now exist worldwide than just a decade ago. These same consumers are eager to work to improve themselves and will work for less money than US workers. This puts somewhat of a lid on wages in this country and thereby helps keep inflation under control.

At the same time the global community is undergoing a revolution in computer technology and communications development. Without question the United States is the acknowledged leader in the technology revolution. Not only has this increased demand for our products worldwide, but it has also led to greater efficiency for US companies that use this technology. It has also led to the creation of companies and industries that would have been inconceivable a generation ago, including internet companies, cellular phone and CD disk manufacturers, software developers and so on.

Another factor, perhaps most important in terms of the actual heights the stock market can attain, is the maturation of the baby boom generation from consumers to savers and investors. This was the first truly college-educated generation. Many boomers have high paying jobs or are of an entrepreneurial bent, and many are past the mortgage paying and kids-in-college period. The extra money that used to be spent on such things is now going into IRAs, retirement accounts and brokerage accounts. And these people have another 10 to 15 years of productive work ahead of them. This should seem to bode well for the stock market.

Another factor aiding this bull market is the improvement in our government's annual budget from deficit to surplus. How much faith we can put in the numbers coming out of Washington (Social Security and Medicare are still vital concerns) could be the subject of another book, but I shall not get into that discussion here. What is important for the stock market are the numbers reported in the media. These show deficit reduction leading to surplus over the past several years, and this development has occurred, at least in part, to tax receipts on realized capital gains from the roaring stock market. If the budget surplus continues into the early years of the new millennium, this should continue to be bullish for stocks. A surplus, or even a balanced budget, should be perceived as non-inflationary which should lead to lower long-term interest rates which in turn would cut the cost of borrowing for companies (and individuals alike). Continuing surpluses should also eventually lead to tax cuts which would be very bullish for stocks.

In addition to these other considerations, our economy is still the number one economy in the world and our dollar is still the world's reserve currency. Especially with the fall of the former Soviet Union, the United States remains the premier military power in the world. Mainland China could challenge in terms of manpower but probably will not be able to match the US in terms of military technology for at least another decade or two. All these factors favor a bull market.

On the negative side, one often hears the possibility of a "shock." This could take the form of terrorism or war or scandal or shortage of some commodity, in particular oil. None of these scenarios have a zero probability of occurring. Our country has already experienced several episodes of domestic terrorism, including the World Trade Center and the Oklahoma City bombings. So far these incidents have been isolated and contained. Worldwide the probability of terrorist attacks is even higher. Could terrorism really affect the US stock market? Yes, if the situation became serious enough. Investors could lose faith in the ability of governments to control circumstances, which in turn could cause them to lose faith in financial institutions and paper assets. A shift to hard assets might result.

Similar arguments could be made if a major war were to erupt. I think that investors sometimes forget that we are not that many years away from the Iraq/Persian Gulf War and that today there are even more hot spots around the world. The Middle East is still very explosive, and as one moves from the Balkans to Greece and Turkey, then to Georgia, Chechnya, Azerbaijan, Turkmenistan, Afghanistan, and to Pakistan and India it is easy to see there exist many regional conflicts and much political instability. Russia remains unstable both economically and politically and it being further burdened by revelations of government corruption. To top if off, mainland China is flexing its military muscle by firing missiles over Taiwan's airspace and rattling sabers over the oil-rich Spratly Islands. The threat of major war sometime in the first decades of the new millennium is real.

The specter of scandal hung over the Clinton administration almost from its first day in office. However, the Clinton White House showed great skill in maneuvering around many embarrassing issues. However, future scandals involving the White House or Congress may not be so deftly contained. Any illegality on the part of either the executive or legislative branches could have the domino effect of collapsing confidence in our government, the dollar, the US bond market and the US Stock markets. It would make sense in such a scenario especially for foreign investors, but for domestic investors as well, to shift assets out of US markets and into markets with a more stable political background.

Another oil shortage would be a major shock to the economy. Shortages of other commodities could also be detrimental, but none would have the effect oil would. The introduction of billions of new consumers on the world marketplace, both due to the collapse of communism and the emergence of the developing countries, has already increased the demand for oil by several million barrels a day. Increased demand is expected to continue for many years forward. The slightest disturbance in the flow of oil, to say nothing of a major war in an oil-producing region, would dramatically increase the price of oil. This is turn would increase the prices of almost everything for American companies and for American consumers, leaving them effectively with less money to spend. This would be extremely bearish for our stock market. An interesting book that discusses the importance of oil is Robert Czeschin's *The Last Wave* (see References at the end of this chapter).

There are other factors that could derail the US stock market. Some pundits argue, quite convincingly, that what has kept US interest rates low in the 1990s in the face of a five-trillion-dollar-plus total government acknowledged debt burden, is the continued buying by foreigners, and in particular foreign central banks, of our treasury debt. As the new millennium begins the total holdings of US treasuries by foreign central banks is over 600 billion dollars. It is thought that China holds about $150 billion in US government obligations. Treasury holdings by foreign financial institutions and foreign nationals would add to this figure. The question that begs being asked is: what if even a fraction of the foreign money invested in US debt were repatriated, regardless of the reason for the repatriation? Who would come forward to purchase this debt? Chances are that the extra supply would force down the price of US Treasuries, thereby increasing interest rates. US government officials, Federal Reserve officials and Wall Street executives argue this would never happen, but….

Another negative factor is that during the 1990s the American consumer has been stretched to the limit with personal debt. The percentage of disposable income going to pay off debt is at an all time high. Credit card delinquencies and personal bankruptcies have increased dramatically. All this bodes ill for continued high consumption by Americans. This could mean lower sales for US companies, which in turn implies lower earnings and a decrease in share price.

There also exist a number of negative technical considerations. One is that the Dow Jones Industrials have not undergone a market pullback of 20% since 1987. In historical terms this is very unusual. A second is that the average P/E of the S&P 500 is now around 30. This is thought to be quite high. Another that is worrisome to many market pundits is the average yield on the S&P 500 Index. It has fallen to well under 2%, the lowest in market history. Markets were once considered overvalued if the yield on the S&P 500 fell to 3%. Many other indicators also point to an overvalued market.

The fair value of the stock market in the year 2000 is anybody's guess. I argue elsewhere in this guide that prices since the late 1960s have increased in value by approximately 6.5 times. The Dow first reached the 1,000 level in 1966. It declined significantly from there (to 736) but approached that 1,000 level again (to 995) in late 1968 then declined to 627 in 1970. It would rise moderately above 1,000 in 1973, 1976 and 1981. Finally in late 1982 it would finally break loose and never again return to below 1,000. But for 16 years, during some of our nation's worst inflation, the Dow essentially went nowhere. You can argue that the Dow at 1,000 in 1966 and 1968 was overvalued, but if you apply my inflation factor of 6.5 to the Dow of that period, you come up with a value of 6,500. Is this a fair value? I don't know, only that it would correspond to the increase in prices of other goods and services. But the Dow has already been as high as 11,700. So have stocks gone too far and are we near the end of this bull market? I don't know. Often markets tend to overshoot their fair value, sometimes by a significant amount. If the Dow overshot my "fair value" by 100% we would be looking at a Dow of 13,000.

So there you have it. Bull or bear. The arguments on either side are compelling. What ultimately drives markets, however, is liquidity (money) and psychology. If investors and institutions have money they will invest in stocks. The low interest rate climate has fueled liquidity for a number of years. There are factors that could change this situation, but so far they have not materialized. The major indices continuously hitting new highs has bolstered investor confidence. But there are two components to investor psychology: greed and fear. Any of the shocks discussed above could rapidly create a loss of confidence and a result-ant stampede out of stocks.

References

1. William J. O'Neil, *How to Make Money in Stocks,* McGraw-Hill, New York, NY, 1988.

2. Peter Lynch, *One Up on Wall Street*, Penguin Books, New York, NY, 1989.

3. Martin Zweig, *Winning on Wall Street*, Warner Books, New York, NY, 1990.

4. Norman G. Fosback, *Stock Market Logic,* Dearborn Financial Publishing, Inc., Fort Lauderdale, FL,1992.

5. Jeffery B. Little and Lucien Rhodes, *Understanding Wall Street*, Liberty Hall Press, an imprint of McGraw-Hill, New York, NY, 1991.

6. Sam Stovall, *Sector Investing,* McGraw-Hill, New York, NY, 1996.

7. Charles B. Carlson, *Buying Stocks without a Broker*, McGraw-Hill, New York, NY, 1992.

8. Robert W. Czeschin, *The Last Wave*, Agora Books, Baltimore, MD, 1992.

9. Jack D. Schwager, *Market Wizards*, Harper & Row, New York, NY, 1989.

10. Jack D. Schwager, *The New Market Wizards*, HarperBusiness, New York, NY, 1992.

11. James K. Glassman and Kevin A. Hassett, *Dow 36,000*, Times Business/ Random House, New York, NY, 1999.

12. David Elias, *Dow 40,000*, McGraw-Hill, New York, NY, 1999.

13. Charles W. Kadlec, *Dow 100,000 Fact or Fiction*, New York Institute of Finance, New York, NY, 1999.

14. Peter Schwartz, Peter Leyden and Joel Hyatt, *The Long Boom*, Perseus Books, Reading, MA, 1999.

15. John Steel Gordon, *The Great Game*, Scribner, New York, NY, 1999

16. Todd G. Buchholz, *Market Shock*, HarperBusiness, New York, NY, 1999.

Chapter 5

Who Owes You What?

The return on your principal is not as important as the return of your principal.

Will Rogers

Debt instruments make up the largest financial markets in the world. From US treasuries to the debt of foreign governments, corporations and municipalities to the packaging of mortgages and car loans and credit card debt, these instruments come under the general heading of **debt securities,** or more loosely as bonds. They are, in fact, IOUs—a statement of how much is borrowed (or owed) and the conditions under which payment will be made. Note that if you purchase an institution's debt security you become a **creditor** of that institution. In contrast, if you buy a company's stock, you take an equity (or ownership) position in the company, and your stock is called an equity security.

For US government debt, or **treasuries,** the following distinctions are made depending on the length of maturity. For debt instruments expiring in a year or less the IOUs are called treasury bills or **T-bills;** over one year to ten years, **treasury notes;** over ten years (usually 30 years), **treasury bonds** or "long bonds." If you hear about "the long bond," this refers to the latest issue of the US 30-year bond. With the acknowledged US government debt well over five trillion dollars, you begin to realize what a huge financial market this is. Add in the debt of all other countries, all corporations and municipalities, to say nothing of mortgages and other consumer debt and the scope of this market becomes mind boggling.

In this guide I cannot possibly cover every type of debt security. I will concentrate on what is generally referred to as the **bond market**. I will first try to give you a feeling for this market, for how these securities are priced and where to find information on them. Then I will cover US government debt in more detail and briefly discuss corporate and municipal debt.

The Language of Bonds

Each investment class has its own jargon, but to me the jargon of bonds has always been a little more arcane. Maybe it's a holdover from those elementary school days when we brought in our quarters to save up for US Savings Bonds. I mean, even then, in simpler times and round-numbered interest rates eras, who could figure out what your real rate of return was and when you could actually spend the thing on a new bicycle? What we now know is that US Savings Bonds were the predecessors of zero coupon bonds, defined later.

To complicate matters further for someone like me who is trying to describe bonds, most institutions no longer issue engraved certificates. Rather, the bonds are registered in the holder's name with interest payments sent automatically. The Treasury Department stopped issuing certificates after the first trillion or two of debt piled up and now uses a system where all securities exist only as bookkeeping entries (I describe later how to purchase US treasuries directly). Actually, you most likely will purchase your bonds through a broker anyway so your securities will be in the broker's name just as your stocks are in "street name." Your account will indicate your ownership of the bonds and will get credited with the interest payment.

Allow me for a moment to return to that era when bond certificates were actually issued. In addition to the name of the borrower this certificate would indicate the par value, the interest rate and the date of maturity. The **par value** is simply the amount due the bondholder when the "loan" is completed. This amount is usually in multiples of $1,000 for corporates and government notes and bonds (municipal bonds are usually in multiples of $5000). The **interest rate** is the percentage of par value paid each year to the bondholder. It remains fixed during the life of the bond (unless the bond interest rate is floating based on an index of some sort). The **date of maturity** is the year the loan is due and the par value is to be returned to the bondholder.

As I write this paragraph I'm perusing the **Money and Investing** section of my *Wall Street Journal* and I see under New York Exchange Bonds that AT&T has several listed. One is the AT&T bond of 2004 with an interest rate of 6¾%. This is listed as: ATT 6¾04. Everything you need to know in one compact expression. AT&T has another bond due in 2005 with an interest rate of 7%. It is listed as: ATT 7s05. Here the "s" has no meaning. It is used, since there is no fraction in this case, to separate the interest rate from the year.

When bond certificates were actually issued they came with coupons attached. The bondholder would clip the coupon and send it in to receive the interest payment. Whoever had possession of the bond could send in the coupon, hence the name "bearer bonds." The next time you see a spy thriller involving bearer bonds, you'll know where the expression came from. A carryover from these certificates is that even today people refer to the interest on a bond as its **coupon**.

Corporate and municipal bonds often include a **call** provision. Such bonds are said to be **callable**. A call gives the borrower the right to repay the principal well in advance of the maturity date, though usually not before a fixed number of years. The usual reason for such a redemption is so the borrower can refinance at a lower interest rate. This action obviously does not favor the bondholder. Treasury bills, notes and bonds usually do not have call provisions.

Most previously issued bonds are freely traded in what is called the **secondary market**. This is where you as a whole investor will most likely buy and sell your bonds. Many new issues are gobbled up by institutions and brokerage houses, anyway, so the small investor has little chance at buying those. A question you might ask is: Why trade bonds? Because bond prices change. Why do bond prices change? Because interest rates change. Why do interest rates change? For many reasons, including inflationary and deflationary pressures.

As an example, suppose you purchased a corporate bond from XXX company at par value ($1,000) and 8% interest. Suppose inflation is tame and a few years later interest rates fall to 6% on newly issued bonds. Clearly your bond is more desirable in the new interest rate environment since it is paying $80/year in interest and the new bonds are paying only $60/year. The price of your bond should rise in value to reflect this new interest rate. Another way to look at this situation is to ask the question: what should my bond value be at 6% interest to return $80 a year? A simple division ($80/0.06) gives $1,333.34. In actual trading your bond may only sell for $1,300. The **current yield** on your bond would then be 6.2% (80/1300 rounded).

If inflation again reared its ugly head, perhaps newly issued bonds would have a 10% interest rate. In that case the new bonds are more desirable than your 8% bonds. The price of your bond would fall in value to reflect the higher interest rate. Again ask the question what bond value at 10% interest rate would return $80. This time the calculation ($80/0.10) gives $800. If the bond actually sold for only $775 then its current yield would be 10.3%.

Note that if you were on the other side of the sale in the above examples, you might be interested in the **yield to maturity**. This is the total rate of return of a bond held to maturity taking into account both interest payments and capital gain or loss on the security. For example, in the first example if you paid $1,300 for a bond and held it to maturity you would end up with a $300 capital loss on the transaction, because at maturity you receive the par value ($1,000) which is always fixed. In the second example if you had paid $775 for the bond, your capital gain at maturity would be $225. In general, the yield to maturity is rather complicated to calculate, but yields are usually quoted as a "yield to maturity" unless designated as a "current yield." In a similar fashion, **yield to call** is the total rate of return including interest payments and capital gain/loss assuming a callable bond will be called on its first call date.

If, indeed, you are buying or selling bonds in the secondary market, you will become aware immediately that **accrued interest** is part of the transaction. If you are buying a bond in between coupon dates, then you will have to pay the present owner for the interest built up or accrued between the last coupon date and the date of purchase. This interest you pay will be recovered on the next coupon date. The accrued interest you pay should be deductible from other interest earned on your tax return (always consult a tax expert on such matters). If you are selling a bond between coupon dates, then you will receive the accrued interest on the date of sale. This interest will likely be reportable on your tax return (see below for interest exemption on municipal bonds), and thus the actual date you sell your bond may be important to you with regard to tax consequences.

I end this section by defining **zero-coupon bonds**. These are bonds which in the days of certificates would have had no coupons attached. That's right—you're catching on—these bonds have no periodic interest payments, much like US Savings Bonds. Instead, they are sold at a deep discount to par value, allowing interest to accrue until maturity at which time the bondholder receives the full par value. In bond listings these bonds will appear with no interest rate component but rather with the symbol **zr**. For example, Motorola has a zero-coupon bond due in 2013. Its listing is Motrla zr13. There is nothing wrong with zero-coupon bonds except unlike US Saving Bonds you are required to report the interest each year, and this can be complicated to calculate. This is the reason most people recommend zero-coupon bonds be placed in an IRA or other tax deferred account.

Specific Bond Purchases

As I've already indicated, the variety of debt securities is almost mind boggling. As a beginner in the bond market, I recommend that you stay away from exotic or creative varieties. Instead stick with the most liquid and most stable securities. These include US treasuries, top-rated corporate bonds and some municipal bonds. I'll briefly discuss each group below. My own preference, in fact, is to stay with treasuries and corporate bonds, but I include municipal bonds because of their special tax exemptions.

This is not to say there are no other attractive and interesting possibilities available, but learn your way around in these debt markets before you begin looking for that extra basis point of interest. One area where I've had some success is the foreign government bond market. However, before you dive into this arena make sure you understand the currency risk (see Chapter 8 on The Color of Money…). In one instance I barely got back in interest payments what I lost in currency devaluation. In every case of a high interest rate, you can be certain there is a reason for it. Institutions, no matter their size or location, will not pay any more interest than the market requires.

US Treasuries

These include T-bills, treasury notes and bonds. These securities are not rated because they are considered risk-free, being backed by the full faith and taxing power of the US government. What this means is that you are sure to receive interest payments and par value at maturity. In the secondary market, however, the prices of these securities do fluctuate, and especially in the case of longer term maturities can deviate substantially from par value.

Though you will most likely want to buy treasuries though your brokerage account, it is possible to buy these securities directly from the Treasury Department. In fact, you can set up your own account through a system called Treasury Direct which is managed by The Bureau of the Public Debt. You set up the account by submitting a PD F 5182 "New Account Request," which you obtain directly from the Bureau or through any Federal Reserve Bank or Branch where you also access your account. The address for the Bureau is:

> The Bureau of the Public Debt
> Information Disclosure Officer
> 999 E Street, NW, Room 500
> Washington, DC 20239-0001

The toll-free number for information on Treasury Direct Electronic Services is (800)-943-6864. If you are plugged into the Internet, you can obtain additional information and request forms at:

> www.publicdebt.treas.gov

Treasury Direct is primarily a bookkeeping system. You cannot redeem your securities before maturity in this system, but you can sell your securities on the secondary market within this system through a program called Sell Direct. If you also have a commercial account you can shift most treasuries back and forth between it and Treasury Direct.

In recent years the Treasury Department has introduced inflation-indexed bonds, called Treasury Inflation Protection Securities, or TIPS. These bonds will have a fixed rate of interest at auction. Semiannual interest payments will be made based on an inflation-adjusted principal recalculated at each payment date, but none of this adjusted principal will be paid out until maturity. The index for measuring the inflation rate will be the non-seasonally US City Average All Items Consumer Price Index for all Urban Consumers (CPI-U) published by the Bureau of Labor Statistics. Honest.

I see several problems with these inflation-indexed bonds. First, you have to trust what the government says with regard to the inflation level. Second, you will have to pay taxes up front on the gain in your adjusted principal. This means, if you hold 10-year notes to maturity, that you will be paying taxes the first year on money you won't see for 9-years, the second year on money you won't see for 8 years, and so on. Though some advisors have been recommending these instruments, I do not see the benefits of them in the low inflation environment of recent years. If you think you want to own these securities I suggest holding them in an IRA or other tax-deferred account.

T-bills: The treasury bill market is the largest debt market in the world. The United States government, the largest debtor nation in the world, is in constant need of refinancing its debt and this market is the primary means of doing so. The maturities of T-bills are 13-week, 26-week and 1-year. Auctions are held every Monday except holidays for 13-and 26-week T-bills and monthly for 1-year T-bills. The minimum bid is $10,000. Above the $10,000 minimum bids can be made in any multiple of $1,000. T-bills are sold at a discount to the face value. In this regard they are identical to zero coupon bonds but are not considered "zeros" because of their short lengths of maturity. Although these securities sell at auction only those bidders planning to purchase $500,000 or more are entitled to make competitive bids. If you were buying direct, say the minimum bid, you would submit your tender form with a $10,000 check attached. After the auction the Treasury Department would then send you an interest check based on the average accepted bid. If this corresponded to say an annual rate of 5%, you would receive a check for $125. After the 3-month period expired, the Treasury Department would send you a check for the principal, $10,000, or credit your Treasury Direct account for this amount.

Some, but not all, financial experts consider T-bills the safest and most liquid securities in the world. Another appeal of T-bills and other treasuries is that the interest income on them is exempt from state and local taxes.

Treasury notes: Notes have maturities of over 1 year up to 10 years. Common maturities in the 1990s are 2-, 5-and 10-year notes. Other maturities used are 3-and 7-year notes. The minimum denomination is $1,000. These securities are issued at or near par value and have coupons. Interest is paid on a semiannual basis. Two-year notes are sold at monthly auctions. Five-year and 10-year notes have recently been auctioned four times a year. Bids are made on a yield basis rather than a discount basis like T-bills.

Treasury notes and bonds trade in points worth $10 each and 1/32nds of a point—or ticks—worth 31.25¢ each. In the bond listings the price of treasury notes and bonds are shown with colons. Thus a price listed as 100:07 would mean 100 7/32 and represent a price of $1002.1875 ($10 per point). A listing of 99:20, which means 99 20/32, represents a price of $996.25.

The risk with regard to market fluctuations in the shorter maturities is considered minimal. The 10-year note, however, can fluctuate substantially in price.

Treasury bonds: Bonds are identical in most ways to notes except their maturities are over 10 years. Although other maturities are possible, when people talk about treasury bonds they are referring to 30-year bonds, or "long bonds." The 30-year bonds recently have been auctioned only twice a year.

The risk in 30-year bonds is considerably higher than with other treasuries. These bonds can fluctuate dramatically in price, both up and down.

The Corporate Bond Market

Corporate bonds are separated into two broad classes, secured and unsecured. **Secured bonds** are backed by the material assets of the issuer. An example is a mortgage bond. **Unsecured bonds** are backed only by the good credit of the issuer who is expected to generate enough cash to pay back both interest and principal. Debentures are unsecured bonds.

The primary feature in this market is that all bonds are rated with regard to risk by either Standard & Poors or Moody's. Corporations, unlike the government, can neither tax nor print money, so some system is needed to differentiate the financial strength of companies. These ratings give a relative assurance of receiving interest payments and the return of principal. I will not define all the possible ratings but only say that Standard & Poors uses an AAA, AA, A, BBB, BB, B, CCC, CC, C system, with a D rating indicating "in default." Moody's uses an Aaa, Aa, A, Baa, Ba, B, Caa, Ca, C system.

Clearly, lower rated bonds will pay much higher interest or sell for much less than par, or both. Junk bonds are defined as "less than investment grade bonds." With that definition all bonds rated BB or lower by Standard & Poors or rated Ba or lower by Moody's fit the junk bond description. Especially for the beginner, I recommend sticking with only the highest rated bonds. Sure, you'll pay more for these bonds and receive less in interest, but recall Will Rogers' warning at the beginning of this chapter.

Maturities for corporate bonds—"corporates"—can be just about anything, with usual lengths ranging from 1-to 20-years. A few companies, including Disney, have in the past several years issued 100-year bonds. Considering the present life expectancy of individuals and that very few companies exist for a century, I would think the purchasers of 100-year bonds have a very optimistic outlook. Remember that corporates often include a call provision.

The usual par value for corporate bonds is $1,000. Occasionally smaller denominations called "baby bonds" are issued. Offerings of corporate bonds are usually purchased by institutions in large quantities, often round lots of $100,000. The secondary market is very active and includes the New York and American stock exchanges and over-the-counter (OTC) trading.

Corporates trade in points worth $10 each and eight's of a point worth $1.25 each. A price of 99 1/8 would represent a bond worth $991.25. A price of 101 3/4 (3/4 = 6/8) would represent a bond worth $1017.50.

The interest on corporate bonds is not exempt from income taxes.

Municipal Bonds

Municipal bonds or "muni bonds" or just "munis" are debt securities of political entities smaller than the federal government. They are used to fund anything from airports and highways to education and hospitals to housing and sports complexes. The market is huge. Munis, like corporates, are rated. Though municipalities generally have limited taxing power, not all entities are equally financially sound. Recall that New York City almost went bankrupt in the mid-1970s. Hence the need for credit analysis of this area of the debt market.

Munis are listed in points and eight's, like corporates, usually under the heading Tax-Exempt Bonds. There are thousands of munis but very few are listed in the business newspapers on a given day.

The usual minimum for muni bonds is $5,000. The maturities vary widely from short term obligations of a few months to 30-years. They can be callable. They can also be issued in "serial" maturities where a set amount of interest and principal is repaid each year. They are traded only over the counter.

The main attraction of munis is that the interest on them is exempt from federal income taxes (unless you have borrowed money to buy them—consult your tax advisor). The interest may also be exempt from state taxes in the state in which the bond is issued. Because of this feature these securities usually pay a lower rate of interest than a corporate bond of comparable risk and maturity. Nevertheless, they may be appropriate to high income earners or high wealth individuals who may benefit from this tax-exemption.

The Interest Rate Story

I wish there were well-known methods for selecting bonds, much as there are for selecting stocks. I am not aware of any. However, there are a number of related factors that you can keep your eye on. These all center around interest rates, and though I've called this section "The Interest Rate Story," the whole story would take volumes. In what follows I will concentrate on US treasuries, since the value of these securities have such a dramatic effect on the overall debt securities market.

You have probably noticed by now from the examples above, or from your general knowledge, that interest rates and the prices of bonds move in opposite directions. As interest rates drop, bond values increase. As interest rates rise, bond values decrease. The real questions are: when are interest rates high or low and what makes them change direction? Believe me, millions of investors worldwide would love to have the magic answers to these questions. Interest rates not only affect the debt securities markets but stock markets as well. This is true because if the return in bonds is high enough, investors will eschew the high risk of the stock market and put their money instead in the relatively lower risk investment class of bonds.

From a position in early 2000, it is now clear that the 1980 yields for treasuries in the mid-teens was high. You can laugh and say, "Sure, anybody can see that," but at the time hardly anybody wanted to buy bonds. The outlook with rapidly rising commodity prices and oil shortages and hostages in Iran was so negative that the US bond market was actually on the verge of collapse. During most of the

1980s and 1990s, with a few blips in between, rates dropped all the way to 3% for T-bills in 1993 and to a low yield of 4.69% on the long bond in 1998. Neither of these numbers represent historic lows, but they may have been the lows in this long bond bull market. The peculiar thing is that in this relatively low interest rate environment, there has been huge interest in our treasuries, especially from foreign central banks who now own over $600 million of our debt.

I wish I could tell you that I understand perfectly why interest rates fell from the 1980 highs to their present lows. I do not. Interest rates and investors' perceptions of them depend on many things, including the strength of a nation's economy, its government's attention to debt levels, the strength of its currency (and visa versa—interest rates affect currencies), the strength of stock markets, current rates of inflation or disinflation, even a nation's military might, and so on.

But something else should come into play, namely supply and demand. Securities are no different than commodities or other "stuff" in this respect. If a company issues additional stock in order to raise working capital, the price of its stock should go down. If an institution issues too many bonds its credit rating will go down and its bonds will decrease in value. This is not what happened with US treasuries. During the 1980s and 1990s the US government issued huge numbers of debt securities (or at least huge numbers of bookkeeping entries). The securities did not go down in price. Their value increased. In other words, interest rates came down.

The situation is similar to your lending money to your uncle, let's call him Sam. He comes to you the first year wanting to borrow $1,000 at 6% interest. He's a fine, upstanding uncle, so you agree. At the end of the first year he brings you $60 in interest but not the principal. He suggests that his needs are vast and, oh yes, could you lend him $2,000 more at 5% interest? Well, he did pay the interest, so you reluctantly agree. At the end of the second year he brings you $60 interest on the first loan and $100 interest on the second loan, but repays no principal.

It seems his needs have increased and he requests a third loan of $3,000 but he only wants to pay 4% interest. At this point, a rational person might balk. You might suggest that if he is not going to repay the principal shouldn't he at least pay more in interest? This was basically the situation with US treasuries in the 1980s and most of the 1990s. Yet investors, foreign or otherwise, did not balk—they piled into this market.

Am I suggesting that interest rates may have been manipulated and should go much higher in the future and that consequently bond prices will decline? No. I don't know the answer to that question. What I am suggesting is that directions of interest rates and their fair values can be confusing. That's why anyone investing in debt securities needs some way to monitor interest rates. The remainder of this chapter is devoted to that pursuit.

Fed Watch

People on Wall Street, in large and small towns in the US and from all around the world try to stay attuned to what the next move by the Federal Reserve, the US central bank in all but name, will be. Bond and stock markets can experience violent reactions merely from a comment by the Federal Reserve Chairman, presently Alan Greenspan, or from one of the other six Board of Governors (seven total counting the chairman) or even from one of the twelve Federal Reserve Bank presidents. Even though the Fed often is simply reacting to market forces, it and particularly Mr. Greenspan assumed an aura of invincibility in the 1990s. Mr. Greenspan is credited with not only magically bringing down interest rates but with keeping inflation in check as well. Not everyone agrees with this interpretation, and for a different view see James Grant's book, *The Trouble with Prosperity* (see References). This book also answers some other questions regarding interest rates. An excellent book on the Fed itself is *Secrets of the Temple* by William Greider (see References). What the Board of Governors does is (1) set reserve requirements and (2) set the discount rate. It also "targets" the federal funds rates.

Reserve requirements refer to the percentage or fraction of demand deposits that a bank must keep in reserve either in currency or as deposits in the Federal Reserve. Note, that within reserve requirements, loans that are redeposited as demand deposits can be loaned again, and in this way an original demand deposit can be multiplied many times. The actual multiplying factor is 1/R, where R is the reserve requirement. If R is 20%, then a demand deposit can be multiplied (lent out) 5 times (1/0.2). If R is only 10%, then a demand deposit can be multiplied 10 times (1/0.1). Thus, by setting R the Fed determines how much money the bank can create. This number is changed grudgingly and only by small amounts. I am not aware of it being changed in the 1990s.

The **discount rate** is the interest rate the Fed charges on loans to commercial banks. The **federal funds rate** (fed funds rate) is the interest rate member banks charge one another for loans. Banks sometimes have to borrow overnight from the Fed's "discount window" or from other member banks as a temporary means of restoring their reserves to required levels. Clearly if this rate is high it costs the banks more to lend and this in turn will cause them to be more cautious with their own lending.

The Fed does not determine the rates on T-bills, notes or bonds. These are determined at auction and in the secondary market. In all fairness, though, the discount rate and fed funds rate have great influence on other interest rates, from the prime rate banks charge to the T-bill rate. In fact, it is not uncommon to see the T-bill rate in the secondary market fluctuate around the fed funds rate. If there is a perceived change in the fed funds rate, the T-bill rate will tend to gravitate in that direction.

One other function of the Fed is its **open market operations** in which it purchases or sells US government securities. This decision is made by the Open Market Committee which consists of the Board of Governors, the president of the Federal Reserve Bank of New York, who is a permanent member, and the presidents of four other Federal Reserve banks on a rotating basis. If the Fed purchases government securities, it increases the money supply which can force interest rates down (the prices of these securities goes up). If the Fed sells US government securities, it decreases the money supply which can force interest rates up.

Now you can be a Fed watcher, too.

The Yield Curve

The yield curve is nothing more than a plot of yields of US Treasuries (the vertical axis) versus the maturity (the horizontal axis). The normal situation is for yields to increase with maturity, though not necessarily in a linear fashion. This kind of plot is called a **positive yield curve**. Sometimes, however, short term interest rates rise above longer term rates. Such a plot is called an **inverted yield curve**. Sometimes interest rates for all lengths of maturity are very close together. Such a plot is called a **flattened yield curve**. You can easily plot these curves with paper and pencil. Save the result. The next time you plot the yield curve compare the graph with the previous one. The direction of interest rates should be clear.

Yield Curves

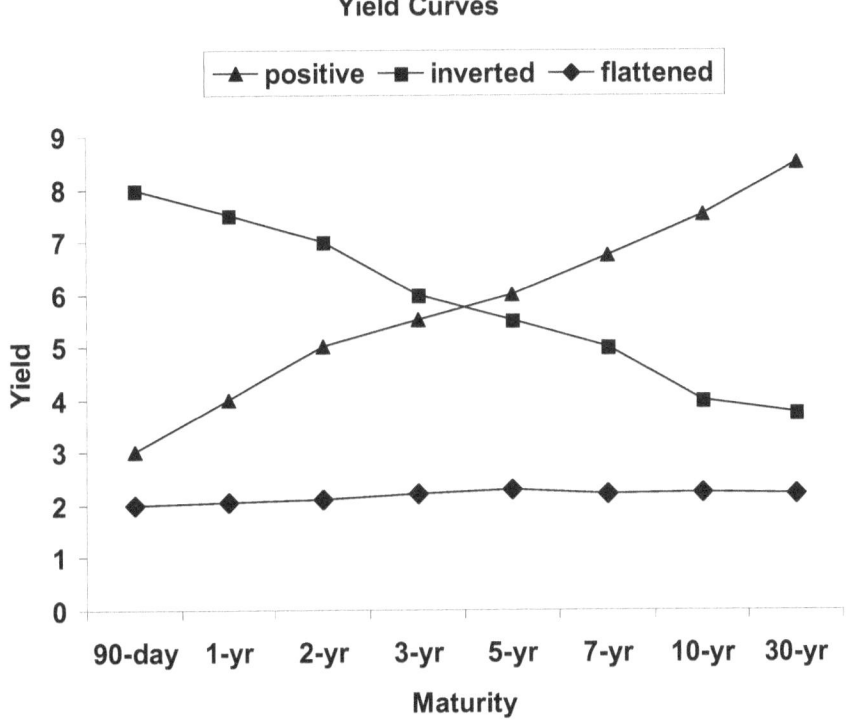

Fig. 5-1

The TED-Spread

The TED-Spread is the difference in interest rates between the 3-month US *T*-bill and 3-month *Euro*dollar deposits. Eurodollars are any deposits of US dollars outside the United States. This includes all deposits of US dollars in foreign banks and financial institutions, in branches of foreign banks on US soil and in US-based banks on foreign soil. It is estimated that well over a trillion Eurodollars exist, but nobody is certain of the exact amount.

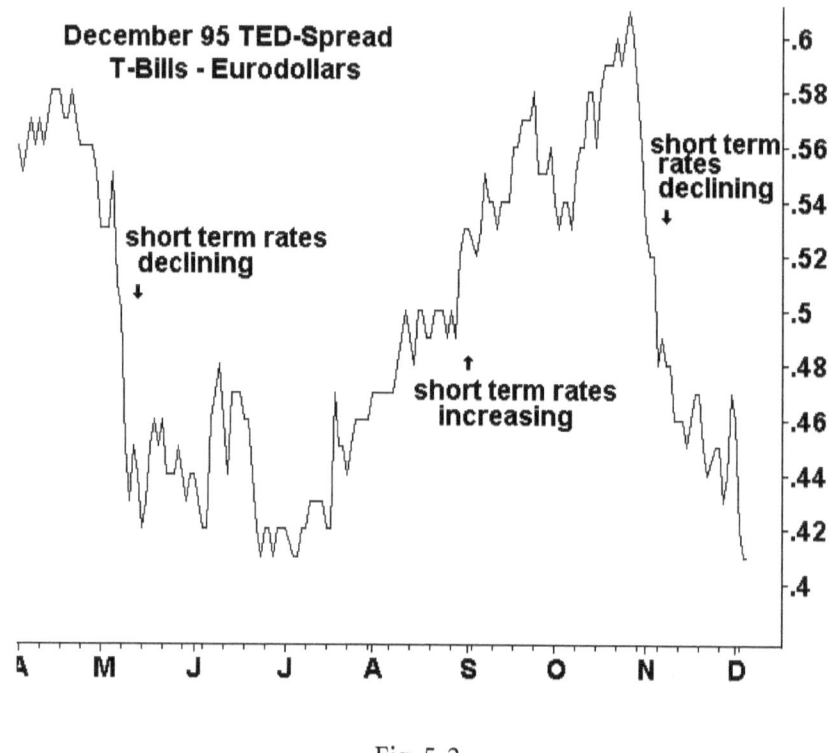

Fig. 5-2

Eurodollar deposits are not backed by the US or any other government which means there is no deposit insurance, only the good faith and credit of the bank. There are no reserve requirements for Eurodollar deposits. There is also the risk that the country in which they are deposited could issue some restrictions or controls on US dollar deposits. Also Eurodollar deposits are usually in the form of CDs and thus are not as liquid as T-bills. These and other considerations force banks to pay higher interest rates on Eurodollar deposits than would be expected on T-bills. In times of stability and low interest rates, the spread is rather narrow. In times of instability and higher interest rates the spread can widen significantly.

The way I follow the TED-Spread is to follow the front month futures contracts for both T-bills and Eurodollars. I show an example in Figure 5-2. I discuss futures contacts in the chapter on "Exotics," but to follow the TED-Spread with futures you need only go to the Commodities section of your business newspaper and subtract the Eurodollar value (given in discount form) from the T-bill value (also given in discount form). You do not need a computer to keep track of the TED-Spread. Furthermore, you probably don't have to track it more than once a week. The key is that if the spread narrows (decreases), the direction of short-term interest rates is down. If the spread widens (increases), the direction of interest rates is up. For much of the 1990s following the TED-Spread has been as interesting as watching paint dry. This doesn't mean we shouldn't be vigilant, however. Remember that short-term rates influence the yields of longer-term debt securities.

The NOB-Spread

This is another interest rate spread, but this one will give you a feel for the direction of longer-term interest rates. NOB stands for *Notes Over Bonds*. More specifically, subtract the price of the 30-year US treasury bond from the price of the 10-year US treasury note.

The basic idea is that if interest rates change, longer-term debt securities will be affected more than shorter-term debt securities. If interest rates fall the 30-year bond will increase in price faster than the 10-year note. Hence the NOB-Spread should narrow (decrease), possibly even turn negative. If interest rates rise the 30-year bond will decrease in value faster than the 10-year note and hence the NOB should widen (increase). Note that it is the direction of the spread, increasing or decreasing, that is of interest rather than the actual value of the spread.

I again use the nearest futures contract for this spread. For note and bond contracts expiring any time up to December 1999, a notional coupon value of 8% had been used to determine values of the underlying notes and bonds. This notional coupon value was changed to 6% with the March 2000 contracts. Starting with the March contacts if yields were exactly 6% the value of the underlying note or bond would be 100 (remember each point is $10). If the yield were less than 6%, the value of the underlying note or bond would be greater than 100. If the yield were greater than 6% the value of the underlying note or bond would less than 100. (Remember yields and prices go in opposite directions.) These details are not crucial to understanding the NOB-spread. Go to the Commodities section of your business newspaper and subtract the nearest contact 30-year bond value from the nearest contract 10-year note value (these will be in points and 32nds of a point). As for the TED-Spread, you can probably get away with doing this once a week. Remember a decreasing spread indicates lower long-term interest rates, an increasing spread indicates higher interest rates. I give an example of this spread in Figure 5-3.

Summary

The debt securities market is the largest financial market in the world. It is also one of the more confusing investment classes because of the jargon used and the variety of instruments available. Don't allow this to discourage you from investing in it. Follow this guide and stick with the most common securities—US treasuries, corporates and munis. Invest in only the highest rated corporates or munis.

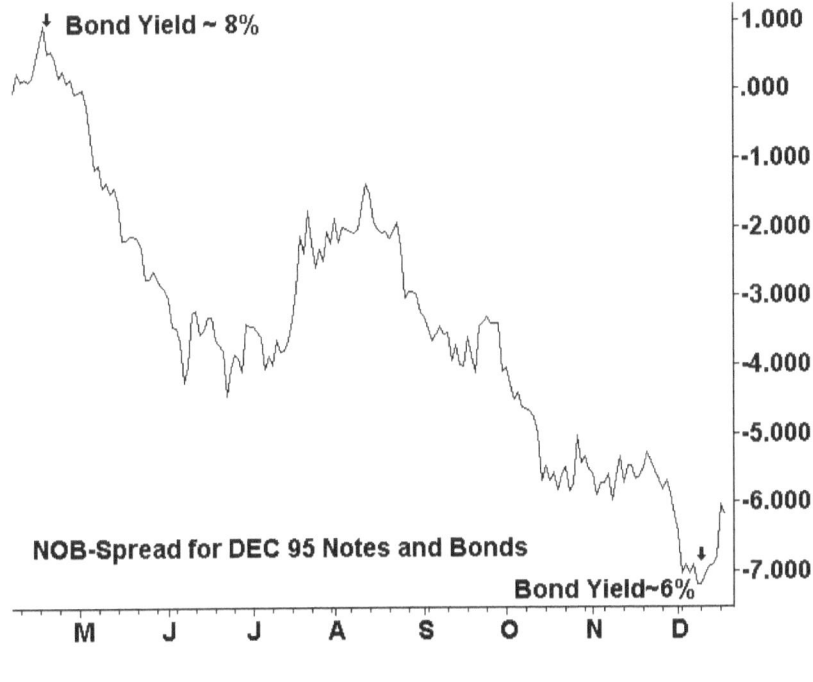

Fig. 5-3.

Understand the inverse relationship between bond prices and interest rates. Keep abreast of interest rate directions by watching the Fed, particularly the discount rate and federal funds rate, by noting the shape of the yield curve, and by tracking the TED-Spread and NOB-Spread. Follow these indicators for a while and it will become second nature as well as an interesting and enjoyable exercise.

References

1. David M. Darst, *The Complete Bond Book*, McGraw-Hill, New York, NY, 1975.

2. Robert Lamb and Stephen P. Rappaport, *Municipal Bonds*, McGraw-Hill, New York, NY, 1987.

3. Donald R. Nichols, *Zero Coupon Investments*, Dow Jones-Irwin, Homewood, IL, 1989.

4. Michael Bowe, *Eurobonds*, Square Mile Books/Dow Jones-Irwin, Homewood, IL, 1988.

5. James Grant, *The Trouble with Prosperity*, Times Books/Random House, New York, NY, 1996.

6. William Greider, *Secrets of the Temple*, Touchstone/Simon & Schuster, New York, 1987.

Chapter 6

Mutuality

A typical conversation with Jimmy Rogers on CNBC, circa 1997:
"How many mutual funds are out there now? About 9,000?"
"Yeah. That's about right," answers the commentator.
"There can't be that many smart 29 year olds, can there?"
Jimmy asks rhetorically, a mischievous smile spreading across his face.

Nine thousand mutual funds? I'm not certain there are that many. If that number were accurate it would represent more funds than there are stocks on the New York, American and NASDAQ stock markets combined. I've read elsewhere that there are over 7,000 funds. In any case, these kinds of numbers should give any mutual fund investor pause. When any investment sector is hot, as stocks and mutual funds have been through most of the 1980s and 1990s, both investors *and* fools rush in. Oil and gold come to mind in the late 1970s. People thought that oil would go to $50 a barrel and stay there. It subsequently fell to $10 a barrel. People who bought gold at over $800 an ounce thought it would continue to rise into the stratosphere. Gold has subsequently fallen to as low as the $250 range. Real estate, especially in the Southwest and California, was hot from the 1970s into the late 1980s when it collapsed along with the savings and loan industry. Am I suggesting that mutual funds are about to collapse? Well...what I *am* suggesting is that mutual funds are **hot, hot, hot!** That in itself should raise some cautionary flags about the stock market and the mutual fund industry. The variety of funds itself is mind-boggling, ranging from blue chip and index funds to aggressive growth and sector funds to global stock and specific country funds to government securities and high yield (junk bond) bond funds.

Does this all sound like I'm negative on mutual funds? Not at all. I have owned mutual funds and continue to own a few mutual funds as part of my investment portfolio. I park cash in money market mutual funds. However, I am not as enthusiastic as the general investing public. One reason is that I prefer to do my own investing. I prefer to own individual stocks or bonds rather than mutual funds. Before this chapter is over, I'm going to introduce you to an entirely different concept in mutual fund investing. But first allow me to discuss some aspects of buying and owning mutual funds that everyone investing in this area should be aware of.

In the last sentence I used the word "area" and not the phrase "investment class." I do not consider mutual funds a distinct investment class, and because of this I do not intend to spend a great deal of time on this subject. If you are invested in a stock mutual fund then that investment is, strictly speaking, a part of your stock portfolio. If you are invested in a bond mutual fund then that investment is part of your bond portfolio. If you are invested in a money market mutual fund then that investment is part of your cash portfolio. The biggest advantage of mutual funds is that you are automatically diversified in that portion of your portfolio. Your entire portfolio should still be diversified as defined previously and as I will continue to stress throughout this guide.

Closed-end Funds and Open-end Funds

You should be aware of the two broad categories of mutual funds. **Closed-end funds** trade on the stock exchanges, just like ordinary shares of a listed company, and have a fixed number of shares. The difference is that a closed-end fund will own the shares of many companies and is itself the owner of these shares. If you buy a closed-end fund, you own shares of the mutual fund, not shares of the companies in the fund. Note that you will need a brokerage account to buy or sell shares of a closed-end fund. A closed-end fund can sell at a discount or at a premium. If it is at a **discount** that means the value of the fund is selling for less than the value of the underlying shares it owns. Closed-end funds often trade at a discount because of the management fees charged to operate the funds. If a fund is at a **premium**, it is selling for more than the value of the underlying shares it owns. For example, if a fund has a good track record, is in either a hot sector or owns shares of companies from a country whose own stock market is hot, then investors may be willing to pay more than the total value of the underlying shares. In most cases it is recommended that an investor buy when a fund is selling at a discount, but in all cases you should investigate whether a fund is at a discount or premium—and the reason why—before buying.

The other broad category of mutual funds is the **open-end fund**. It is called open-end because there is no fixed number of shares in these funds. As investors pour more money into these funds, the fund manager simply issues more shares and uses the money to purchase more shares of stock or more bonds, etc., for the fund. Fidelity's Magellan Fund grew to over $100 billion in this way.

Open-end funds are either no-load funds or load funds. **Load funds** have either up front charges (front-end load) or charges when you redeem (back-end load). If you deal with a financial advisor, you may never have heard of a no-load fund. Part of the fee on a front-end load fund goes to pay the financial advisor for "selling" the fund. If you've dealt with a financial advisor and bought mutual funds from him, ask him why he's never suggested a no-load fund. Then watch with delight as he contorts and explains why load funds are so much better. In general, they are not any better. So why pay him and the mutual fund company a hefty chunk of your investing capital? If you pay a 5% front-end load, your fund has to make 5.3% just for you to break even. Plus you lose the investment potential of 5% of your money. I'm sorry, but I cannot condone buying load funds. If you are going to deal with open-end mutual funds stay strictly with no-load funds. I will help you get started with the 800-numbers of several of the best known and best run companies.

The Prospectus

A prospectus is that 3¾" x 8½" mutual fund brochure, which when unfolded doubles in size but which, unfortunately, does not double in clarity. The prospectus is supposed to outline the objectives and expenses of the fund and give you some indications of your rights as an investor. On the application, usually above your signature should be a statement that reads something like the following: "By signing this application, I certify that I have received, read and agree to the terms of the prospectus for each fund in which I am investing." It seems fairly obvious that not all people who sign mutual fund applications have read the prospectus. In this regard the Securities and Exchange Commission recommended a few years ago a new rule that will give investors the choice of receiving a shorter "profile prospectus" or the longer forms being used. I have not heard anything about the profile prospectus lately.

You should read the prospectus. It is the contract between you, the buyer, and the mutual fund. One important section should include information on fund expenses. This is broken down into shareholder transaction expenses, which for a no-load fund should all be "none," and the annual fund operating expenses which are based on a percentage of net assets. These expenses can include management fees, investment advisory fees, shareholder accounting fees, 12b-1 fees, distribution fees and "other expenses." The 12b-1 fees are advertising and marketing fees allowed to be charged against the fund. "Other expenses" could include legal and accounting fees, for example. Not all funds include all these items as part of their operating expenses. However, these fees can add up. Typical total expenses range between 1-2%, with some specialized funds a little higher. I suggest that if the fees are much higher than 2.5% of net assets, you might do well looking elsewhere to invest. As a comparison, the expenses for Vanguard funds, the lowest cost family of funds, is typically well under 1%.

Another important section is the fund's financial information. Here you can examine the per share data for past years (remember, not all funds have been around very long). This should give you an idea of how the fund has performed as well as the history of expenses incurred.

As you move on through the prospectus, you will find out about the fund's investment objectives, policies, practices and limitations and get a general description of the investments themselves. A prospectus typically does not discuss specific investments. You need an annual or semiannual report for that information, and I strongly recommend obtaining one of these.

It is stated in the financial media that the most important factor in a mutual fund's performance is the fund manager. Indeed, in the nineties some of these people have become household names, but with thousands of funds available obviously not all managers have. Nevertheless your prospectus should give you a description of the management of the fund and the names and backgrounds of investment advisors.

The prospectus also should have information about how dividends, capital gain distributions and taxes are handled and how the share price is determined. Capital gain distributions are the topic of the next section.

The last sections of the prospectus tell how to purchase shares of the fund, how to exchange or redeem shares and describe other shareholder services. An important consideration discussed is choosing a distribution option. Most funds give three choices:

(1) Automatic Reinvestment Option—both dividends and capital gains distributions reinvested in additional fund shares.

(2) Cash Dividend Option—dividends paid in cash and the capital gains distributions reinvested.

(3) All Cash Option—dividend and capital gains distributions paid in cash.

Any of these options are acceptable, but the first two can lead to accounting headaches. None of these methods avoid taxes in the year the dividends and capital gains distributions are received, unless, of course, the fund resides inside a tax-deferred vehicle, such as an IRA. Any money in options (1) or (2) that is used to purchase additional shares is thus, in effect, already taxed and thus represents new principal added to your account. To avoid being double taxed when you finally redeem your shares, you must keep track of all this reinvestment money and add it to your other investments (initial investment plus any monthly or other gross purchases) in the fund.

I'm not saying you shouldn't choose options (1) and (2), because these are the best ways to build up the value of your fund. The broad ownership of funds is forcing companies to keep track of these reinvestments for you. But you should be aware of this accounting problem. Other dividend reinvestment programs, including DRIPS (see Carlson in References at end of Chapter 4), have this same accounting dilemma.

So now you see that if you dissect a prospectus, it's not so formidable after all. Even if the shorter versions eventually appear, you can cough slightly away from the telephone and then politely say, "But I prefer the longer one—and an annual report, too."

The Year-end Buying Trap—Be Careful

I admit it. With one of the first mutual funds I bought, I fell right into the year-end capital gain distributions trap. Capital gain distributions have nothing to do with the gain you might receive when you actually sell your shares of a fund. **Capital gain distributions** are the sum of profits and losses that the fund manager realizes by selling holdings in the fund portfolio. These net realized profits are passed along to shareholders and are reportable each year on your income tax return. This is true whether you reinvest the capital gains distribution or receive the proceeds in cash.

Capital gain distributions can be declared more than once a year, but most funds declare near the end of a calendar year. An unfortunate tax consequence can arise as follows. Suppose you buy shares of a fund the day before capital gain distributions are declared. The following day the money you invested is split into principal in the fund plus net realized profits that are tax reportable. It doesn't matter when you invested in the fund, only that you own shares of it on the day the distribution occurs. You don't lose money on the actual day of the distribution, because the capital gains distribution is paid back to you either in additional shares purchased through reinvestment or in cash. But the following April 15 you now have to pay taxes on money that in effect never participated in any real gains but was used merely to purchase new shares of a mutual fund.

This sounds ridiculous and unfair, but it's true. To avoid this situation late in the year, find out when capital gain distributions will be declared and hold off purchasing your mutual fund shares until after that date. Alternatively, hold off new purchases until the first of the year. You can also check whether capital gain distributions are made at other times of the year and plan your purchases around those dates accordingly.

Capital gains distributions used to be split into long term gains and short term gains. I suspect because of the broad ownership of mutual funds this has been simplified, and all capital gains distributions are now treated as long-term capital gains.

Professional Mutual Fund Management

It may or may not surprise you to find that many mutual fund investors do not receive the returns that are touted by the mutual fund industry. One reason for this is that investors tend to hop from one hot fund to another. A fund with spectacular performance one year does not necessarily perform well the following year. This can be due to the cyclical nature of the market sector the fund invests in or for other reasons. Another problem is simply the thousands of funds from which to pick—it is easy for a new investor to become bewildered in this maze and naturally to gravitate to the latest hot fund.

A few years ago *Forecasts and Trends*, a newsletter of ProFutures Financial Group, Inc., reported on the following studies. Apparently the results of these studies were not widely distributed and I did not see them elsewhere. The first was a study commissioned by Marty Zweig—editor of *The Zweig Forecast* and president of Zweig Funds—and published by Morningstar, one of the best-known mutual fund rating services. The study revealed that while the average stock growth fund did very well over the five-year period ending June 1994, the average investor in those same funds *lost* money. A study by Fundminder, Inc., a mutual fund advisory firm, and Morningstar concluded that for the six years 1989-1994 the average stock growth fund returned a compound **12%** average per annum (net of all fees) but the average investor in those same funds gained **only 2%** average per year. Morningstar also did a study of 257 bond mutual funds for the five years ended 1994 and found that while the bond funds averaged **8%** compound per annum (net of all fees), the average investor in them gained **only 1%** average per year. The timing of the average investor is obviously not very good.

It seems clear why the mutual fund industry was not interested in having the results of these studies widely disseminated. Gary Halbert, President and CEO of ProFutures was so appalled by these results that he decided to do something about it. His company conducted a study of mutual fund advisors, professional money managers who will select mutual funds for clients and who move money in and out of the market periodically to reduce volatility. It is these people's business to study the thousands of mutual funds in existence. Most of these advisors, who number in the hundreds across the country, have no need to advertise their services.

The results of this study found a handful of advisors who have beaten the market averages consistently over a long period of time and with considerably less downside risk. Mr. Halbert subsequently made arrangements with some of these top advisors to allow him to offer their services to the clients of ProFutures. At the beginning of 1997 the program was launched nationally and is now available under the name *ADVISORLINK*. The minimums for different advisors range from $10,000 to $100,000. If you are investing in mutual funds in any big way, I believe you owe it to yourself to investigate this service further. As with any investment, do not plunge in until you read all materials and understand them thoroughly. To get an *ADVISORLINK* application kit, contact ProFutures at:

ProFutures Capital Management, Inc.
11612 Bee Cave Road
Austin, TX 78733
(800)-348-3601
mail@profutures.com

Though at present I am not a client of *ADVISORLINK*, I have dealt with ProFutures for a number of years and have found them to be a high quality organization.

Investing with Funds

There exists a specific investment technique called "sector investing" that is most conveniently performed with mutual funds. Because this technique is somewhat more esoteric and may not appeal to everyone, I present a slightly longer, more detailed discussion of it in Appendix 1.

References

Go to the business section of your local bookstore and you will find dozens of books on mutual funds. But make sure you read the book by John C. Bogle, former chairman of The Vanguard Group.

1. John C. Bogle, *Common Sense on Mutual Funds*, John Wiley & Sons, New York, NY, 1999.

2. Norman G. Fosback, Editor in Chief, *Mutual Fund Forecaster*, newsletter of The Institute for Econometric Research, Deerfield Beach, FL (800)-442-9000.

3. Gary D. Halbert, Editor, *Forecasts & Trends*, monthly newsletter of ProFutures, Inc., Austin, TX.

Some Good No-Load Mutual Fund Families

The Vanguard Group
P.O. Box 2600
Valley Forge, PA 19482-2600
(800)-662-7447
www.vanguard.com

The Scudder Funds
P.O. Box 2291
Boston, MA 02107-2991
(800)-225-2470
www.scudder.com

Fidelity Investments
P.O. Box 1284
Boston, MA 02104
(800)-544-8888
www.fidelity.com

Janus Group of Mutual Funds
P.O. Box 173372
Denver, CO 80217-3372
(800)-525-3713
www.janusfunds.com

Chapter 7

Things That Glitter

"In the absence of the gold standard, there is no way to protect savings from confiscation through inflation....Deficit spending is simply a scheme for the 'hidden' confiscation of wealth. Gold stands in the way of this insidious process."

Alan Greenspan, 1966

Should you own gold? Silver? Platinum? Jewelry? Although this depends on individual temperament, for thousands of years sovereign citizens have found it prudent to store a portion of their wealth in precious metals, primarily gold and to a lesser extent silver. Over that time numerous governments and their corresponding currencies have simply ceased to exist. Then, too, there are always the stories of refugees or other unfortunates, immortalized in novels, film or otherwise, whose only wealth they are able to transport with them across borders is a few gold coins. The very thought—though my first impulse is to perish it— to say nothing of the imagery, does make one pause.

There are many reasons for owning things that glitter other than fleeing across borders. All governments throughout history have inflated their currencies, and until the late 1970s and early 1980s gold had been the primary hedge against this tendency. However, with the advent of financial and currency futures and options (see Chapter 9 on Exotics) there has been less need to use gold as an inflation hedge. In fact, for sophisticated investors it is just as easy to short (sell) the dollar or some other currency as it is to buy gold or silver. In fact, taking physical possession of gold or silver can cause its own unique brand of problems. Of course, you can store metals, but this costs money. Even if your hoard is only a couple thousand dollars worth of coins, you don't necessary want to leave that kind of value lying around the house. That implies the necessity of at least a safe deposit box or maybe even a safe. And any significant amount of silver is heavy. A common silver investment is a bag of clad ($1000 face value of pre-1967 Kennedy half-dollars, 40% or 90% silver) which weighs around 60 pounds.

In spite of these considerations I do recommend precious metals as an inflation hedge. Financial futures have not yet withstood the test of time as gold has, and, moreover, most people are not sophisticated investors who want to plunge into or even dabble in the commodity futures markets. Finally, it's not clear how one can monitor a futures contract while fleeing across a border.

Another valid reason for owning things that glitter is the possibility of a major political or economic calamity. I'm not taking here about the necessity of fleeing across borders, but tragic circumstances have the tendency to cause many kinds of assets (especially paper-based) to decline substantially and swiftly. In such instances it could prove prudent to have some assets that would maintain their value if not advance significantly. Again it could be argued that there are other ways to protect against such possibilities, but I again suggest these techniques are best left to professionals. Also in the event that telephone or computer systems are down or clogged (1987 comes to mind), a few coins that one can jingle in a pocket may provide some source of consolation.

There's another reason for investing in things that glitter, and though superficially this may seem to border on the irrational it may be the most important factor in the decision. It is simply the esthetic beauty of the asset. Things that glitter are pretty. Some of the detail on many gold or platinum minted coins almost defies believability. Of course, jewelry, including diamonds and gem stones, need little mention as stores of beauty or sources of admiration.

I will say at this juncture, however, that I do not recommend jewelry as an investment asset or class. It should be considered a luxury and enjoyed as such. It is a poor investment because of the added cost of manufacture and the inherent mark-up at various points of sale. And, of course, many of you will be familiar with the monopoly that DeBeers has on the diamond market, making the true value of that particular item suspect. My knowledge of gem stones borders on ignorance, but I suspect that their value is highly subjective as well.

Precious Metals Investments

So what should you invest in if you want to diversify into "things that glitter?" Without any qualification I recommend gold and platinum coins—silver coins to a lesser extent, unless you have adequate storage facilities and don't mind the extra weight. This preference has nothing to do with my opinion on the fundamentals of the various precious metals markets. All the precious metals have been out of favor for a long time, with minor rallies punctuating rather long term bear markets. Silver may well be the most undervalued commodity of all, not just of the metals, down over 90% in recent years from its all time high. The supply deficit of silver (the amount produced minus the amount used) was about 100 million ounces in 1992 and has exceeded that number every year since. But every time silver tries to advance in price, more supply appears from hoarders, some who bought along with the Hunt brothers during silver's 1980 run at $50 an ounce. If silver has another day in the sun, it is conceivable that it could double, triple or even quadruple from its present value of approximately $5 per ounce. It is unlikely that gold could double or more from its present price near $300/ounce without extraordinary circumstances occurring.

As for specific silver investments I have already mentioned the Kennedy half-dollar clad bags. The 40% clad bags contain approximately 295 ounces of silver and the 90% clad bags approximately 718 ounces of silver. The price you pay will depend on the bullion price for silver plus a premium of around $100 per bag. Expect this premium to increase if the price of silver rises. Other silver coin investments I can recommend are U.S. silver dollars, either the Peace Dollar or the Morgan Silver Dollar, and the Canadian Silver Maple Leaf. All these coins demand substantial premiums over the bullion price, often more than a dollar per one-ounce coin. If you feel these premiums are too high, stick with the clad bags.

Platinum, too, may have better fundamentals than gold in that the two primary producers, South Africa (approximately 70% of world production) and Russia (with approximately 20% of world production) still appear to be extremely unstable as the new millennium unfolds. If one or both of these areas of the world were to erupt into all-out civil war the price of this white metal, platinum, could skyrocket. In addition, the Russians have been dumping both gold and platinum on the world market in order to meet their near-term financial obligations. This condition cannot continue indefinitely. Platinum demand should also continue to rise on the manufacturing front as more and more countries realize the need to control auto emissions, most likely utilizing platinum-based catalytic converters. This metal is also used in electronics, petroleum refining, as a catalyst in many chemical processes, and in dental apparatus. As the Far East continues to prosper the jewelry demand for platinum is likely to increase since the metal is highly valued in that part of the world. And finally, platinum is approximately 15 times more rare than gold. But I digress—these are speculative considerations.

The theme of this chapter is not speculation but rather an investment class that will serve as a store of wealth and protect against unforeseen calamities. As I commented on above I do without qualification recommend precious metals coins, but there's another part to this tale. You should understand the difference between bullion and numismatic coins, especially when making a decision between buying gold or platinum.

Numismatic coins are considered those that have a rarity premium over the bullion price due to their historic significance. Well,...in 1933 Franklin D. Roosevelt in an executive order prohibited the ownership of gold by U.S. citizens, exempting only gold coins of "unusual historic value." Subsequent clarification of who could own these numismatic coins focused on "collectors" as opposed to hoarders, implying it is probably better to own such coins with a variety of dates and mint marks. Also, unusual historic value has come to mean at least a 15% premium over the bullion price.

The ban on gold bullion ownership did not end until the 1970s when Richard Nixon took the dollar off the gold standard, another story altogether. The question anyone contemplating the acquisition of gold coins should consider is: "Could the U.S. government, in this the freest of free countries, ever order the confiscation of gold again?" The answer to this question is not so straightforward. In desperate times governments can confiscate, and have confiscated, anything they want. If gold were confiscated again in the U.S., would the confiscation policies necessarily be the same as in 1933? Nobody really knows.

A better question is: "Why not structure a precious metals investment class to reduce the possibility of confiscation?" While it is true that U.S. Eagles, South African Krugerrands, Canadian Maple Leafs, Austrian Philharmonics and others are beautiful gold bullion coins, a more profound truth is that they are not rare, not numismatic coins. I see nothing wrong with owning a few of these gold bullion coins, but as with other investment classes diversify your holdings—in this case into other metals and into numismatics.

In contrast to gold, platinum has never been used as a monetary unit, even though the coins of various countries do carry a face value.

Confiscation of platinum has not, to my knowledge, ever been the subject of a government decree, nor do those knowledgeable in the precious metals field think such a confiscation is likely. Therefore, although this might not have been something you would have previously considered, I recommend the purchase of platinum bullion coins. The four primary coins available are (in no particular order of preference):

1.   US Eagles
2.   Canadian Maple Leafs
3.   Australian Koalas
4.   Isle of Man Nobles.

All are beautiful coins and all should be available at a small premium—that is if the spot price of platinum is not soaring—(approximately 2-4%) over the bullion price of platinum.

The Rest of the Numismatic Story

When buying numismatic coins you need some additional information. First you should be aware of the different grades of these coins. The higher the quality the coin—in other words, the fewer the imperfections—the higher the grade and the price. In the past each dealer might have his own experts grade coins, and this could lead even in reputable cases to disagreements in value and in disreputable cases to scandal. Since 1986 with the advent of third party grading, such problems have been largely eliminated. The two best known independent grading services are Professional Coin Grading Service (**PCGS**) and Numismatic Guarantee Corporation (**NGC**). Coins graded by these services come encased in a hard plastic case (slabs) with the name of the grading service and the grade of the coin set inside. Tampering with this arrangement should be easily visible.

The grade of numismatic coins ranges from VF30 (VF = very fine) through AU58 (AU = almost uncirculated) to MS/70 (MS = mint state). Coins graded MS/60 or higher are considered uncirculated, i.e., in mint state condition, meaning all lettering, dates and design should be intact. The higher MS numbers have fewer scratches or minor imperfections and as such demand a higher premium. Most uncirculated U.S. numismatic coins are in the MS/60 to MS/65 range. I am not aware of the existence of a MS/70 coin, which I assume represents a state of complete perfection. Because it is costly to grade a coin (this adds about $25 to the premium paid) only the higher-grade coins are usually encased in slabs.

Though numismatic gold from other countries is available and beautiful in its own right I highly recommend that your core numismatic coin collection consist of U.S. coins. There is a large market in these coins, which make them easier to buy and sell. In particular, the two coins I recommend, both known as $20 dollar double eagles are:

1. $20 U.S. Liberties
2. $20 U.S. Saint Gaudens.

The $20 Liberties are further classified into three types:

a) Type 1 Liberties (1850-66) (post gold rush coins); mintage approximately 23.5 million.

b) Type 2 Liberties (1866-76); mintage approximately 16.2 million.

c) Type 3 Liberties (1877-1907); mintage approximately 64.1 million.

Note that the mintage amounts are listed merely as an indication of relative rarity of each type but should not be considered indicative of the number of coins from a given year that have actually survived. Typically with coins of the same grade the older the coin the higher the premium, however, because of the relative scarcity of the Type 2 Liberties, they may hold a higher premium.

The other U.S. numismatic coin of choice is the Saint Gaudens double eagle. It was produced from 1907 to 1933 with some dates such as 1924 and 1927 being much more abundant. The approximate total mintage was 70.3 million coins. The "Saint" is considered to be one of the most beautiful coins ever minted. It was commissioned by Teddy Roosevelt to emulate the beauty of the classic Greek coins on display at the Smithsonian Institute. It was designed by the famous sculptor Augustus Saint Gaudens who died a few months before the first Saints were minted. The coin depicts Liberty holding a torch in her right hand and an olive branch in her left hand, her hair flowing as she strides forward, the sun's rays and the capitol building in the lower background. In my humble opinion you almost need ice in your veins not to get a chill as you admire this coin. The reverse side features the American eagle in flight as it passes in front of the sun's rays.

Both the $20 Liberty and the $20 Saint Gaudens coins have a gold content of 0.96750 ounces. Smaller denomination (hence smaller gold content) U.S. numismatic coins are available, but the premium for an equivalent gold content is greater. I feel its best to stick with the $20 "one ounce" coins.

Though from a collector's viewpoint (as opposed to a hoarder's) it might be desirable to own a variety of grades, I suggest that a good way to buy presumably non-confiscatable gold near the bullion price is to consider non-graded U.S. numismatic coins.

Where can you purchase precious metals bullion coins and U.S. numismatic gold coins? There may likely be a dealer in your city. You may have to pay a little more to buy and sell with a local dealer due to volume considerations or to his having to hunt down the coins for you, but if you can find an honest dealer it may well be worth it to pay this extra premium just to know someone in the business who is close by. Dealers with whom I am familiar and can suggest as a starting point include:

1. Miles Franklin, Ltd.
    3601 Park Center Building, #306
    St. Louis Park, MN 55416
    (800)-822-8080

2. Camino Coins
    851 Burlway Road, #202
    Burlingame, CA 94010
    (800)-348-8001

3. R.W. Bradford & Company
    PO Box 1167
    Port Townsend, WA 98368
    (800)-854-6991

These firms have the best prices I've been able to find. David Schectman at Miles Franklin publishes an excellent newsletter called *The Miles Franklin Report*—I recommend calling them and asking for a free copy. I doubt you will receive better service anywhere than from Bob Sichel and Andy Schectman at Miles Franklin, both of whom bring excellent knowledge and experience to this investing area. Camino, too, offers excellent service and outstanding integrity. Bill Bradford at R.W. Bradford & Company also publishes an interesting newsletter, *Analysis & Outlook*, that can help an investor keep up with the gold, silver and coin markets.

There are probably many other fine coin dealers, but this is an area that has been tainted by fraud and scandal in the past, so be careful out there.

The Precious Metals Markets

What is the fair value that you should pay for your coins? In the case of numismatics—as I have hinted at above—this depends on various factors including rarity, date, grade and current availability (e.g., imagine a huge collection dropping into the lap of a dealer because of an estate liquidation). Then, too, the numismatics market can take on a life of its own, independent of the price direction of the underlying precious metal. Shopping around and experience will tell you what premium you should expect over the bullion price.

Maybe a better question is what is a fair price for the underlying metal. At the turn of the century $20.67 was by law the equivalent of one ounce of gold. Though there were both inflationary and deflationary periods during the 19th century, the dollar maintained its value pretty well over that one hundred year period. Thus I will take $20.67 as a fair price for gold at that time. In 1934 the Gold Reserve Act revalued gold at $35/ounce (and thereby, after gold had been confiscated in 1933, devaluating the dollar by nearly 40%). The U.S. Supreme Court in a ruling involving the Franklin Mint and TWA later confirmed that the legal price of gold should be $42.22, the value still used today by the Federal Reserve to value its gold holdings. There are those who think that is the highest price that the government would have to pay in another confiscation. The point is that even the U.S. government concedes there has been over a 50% devaluation of the dollar since the turn of the century. Others argue that the true purchasing power of the dollar since the turn of the century is about 3 cents. If that were true, then the fair value of gold today would be $689. What I can say with some confidence, since I have lived my adult life through this period is that since the mid-1960s the price of just about everything from automobiles to gasoline to haircuts have increased in dollars terms by at least six to seven times (education and medical services—to list two—even more). Multiplying $42.22, the official price, by 6 yields $253.32. I believe this is the lower limit gold prices should reach.

Interestingly, gold dropped to about $252 in the summer of 1999. I have been recommending purchases. In fact, I believe anywhere between $250 and $350/ounce is a good price to buy gold. On the other hand, should gold somehow rise above $689/ounce as it did in 1979-80, then it is probably overpriced.

As for silver, Bill Bradford (as well as others) argues that the equilibrium price (that price at which the world's silver mines would have to produce as much silver as the world consumes) is between $6.60 and $7.90/ounce. This would seem to imply that silver around $5/ounce is a bargain. Should silver ever make another move up, speculators will probably take it well above its equilibrium level. However, I would not recommend buying silver above $6/ounce.

What about platinum? Here while the fundamental outlook is good, the exact price one should pay is not as straightforward. However, I would use the following guide. Watch the spread in bullion price between platinum and gold (platinum will usually lead gold). If that spread narrows to $50 or less, then the price for platinum is reasonably fair. If this spread widens dramatically, as it most likely will in any speculative buying period in the precious metals, then I would stay away from platinum.

Some Final Considerations

What portion of your investing assets should be allocated to "things that glitter?" It depends on your temperament and level of interest. This is not an investment that you want to be trading frequently. This is a portion of your investment portfolio that you want to keep, perhaps even for your heirs. I believe a minimum of 5% of your portfolio should be devoted to precious metals coins. This can be a sliding scale with higher net worth individuals, depending on their level of interest and enjoyment, putting as much as 15% of their portfolio into this asset class.

A note of caution: coin collecting can become addictive. For all their other attractive features, just remember that coins do not collect interest and their prices can go down. Try to accumulate your coins during dips in the bullion price of the underlying metal and sell only a small portion of your holdings to take some profits when the metals rally substantially.

References

1. Dr. Franz Pick, *The Triumph of Gold*, The Institute for the Preservation of Wealth, Inc., Bethel, CT, 1987.

2. David Schectman, *The Miles Franklin Report* (newsletter), St. Louis Park, MN

3. R.W. Bradford, *Analysis & Outlook* (newsletter), Port Townsend, WA.

Chapter 8

The Color of Money is Green...and Red and Blue and Yellow...

By virtue of living and working in this country, almost all of us are already strategically overexposed to the U.S. economy. Our personal wealth is heavily subject to local wages, local taxes, and local real-estate values. We all reside in the house of the dollar.

Jimmy Rogers, *Worth*

This chapter is about currencies and convincing you to pay attention to their values. Before Richard Nixon took the dollar off the gold standard in 1971, the Swiss franc was worth approximately 25¢, the Deutschemark approximately 27¢, and it took 360 Japanese yen to buy a dollar. In recent years the Swiss franc was worth nearly 90¢, the Deutschemark nearly 70¢, and it took only 80 yen to buy a dollar. Had you been holding money in those currencies during this time, your effective return against the dollar could have been between 250% and 450%. Since the "closing of the gold window" in 1971, when the U.S. currency was no longer convertible into gold, the dollar, though it has had some periods of strength, has lost considerable value against the world's major currencies.

Some of your wealth should be in cash or bonds, and one question I pose here is: "Should all my cash or bonds be in one currency, namely the U.S. dollar?" If you are following the main themes in this book, you know my answer is, "No, all your cash and bonds should not be in one currency. It is prudent, as with your entire investment program, to diversify." Reasons for diversification clearly include hedging against the U.S. dollar but also the possibility for higher returns than those available in dollar denominated accounts. Some higher risk tolerant investors may even want to speculate on the direction of foreign currencies.

Before I go on, let me emphasize that I am *not* a fan of foreign bank accounts. I've owned foreign bank accounts and I know whereof I speak. Although I enjoyed excellent service with my accounts, there were many other disadvantages. First, if you think that owning a foreign bank account will afford you some measure of privacy, consider that if the aggregate value of your foreign bank accounts exceeds $10,000 at any time during a given calendar year you must, under threat of severe penalty, by June 30 of that year file with the Department of the Treasury form TD F 90-22.1, "Report of Foreign Bank and Financial Accounts." So much for privacy. Indeed, rather than providing privacy, foreign bank accounts can actually raise flags for auditors or other suspicious types. If you are holding foreign bank accounts with total value $10,000 or less you can avoid this filing requirement, but then you have to decide whether keeping this smaller amount in a foreign account is worth the hassle. Note that minimum deposits to set up foreign bank accounts can be substantially greater than $10,000.

Second, you cannot escape income tax from interest or other gains derived from a foreign bank account, because the IRS taxes American citizens on their worldwide income. In addition, you may have to pay taxes in the country in which the account is held. This means either applying for a refund—if even allowed—from the host country or filing IRS form 1116 for a foreign tax credit.

Third, the fees on a foreign bank account tend to be exorbitantly high. I know the fees at U.S. banks are rising daily, but they are still lower than those associated with a foreign account.

Fourth, there is usually a language or cultural difference, and this can lead to miscommunications, a deadly circumstance when your investing money is involved.

Finally, there is usually a time difference, and even if you can call your bank directly, who wants to get up at 3:00 a.m. to carry out a simple account transaction? Correspondence by mail creates significant time delays, which can put your foreign investments at a significant disadvantage. Personally I like to have an 800-number I can call during regular business hours.

All this added up, to me, creates far too many headaches to be worthwhile. And for what? So you can have some money outside the U.S.? In times of international turmoil are you really going to be able to get your hands on that money anyway? Holocaust victims or their ancestors fifty years later were still having trouble getting their money out of Switzerland. If the United States with its multi-trillion dollar economy, its five trillion dollar debt and its overwhelming superiority in technology does seriously hit the skids, is there anywhere that will be spared? I know that some newsletter writers promote a so-called Perpetual Traveler (PT) lifestyle, but to whom are these people promoting this? Most of us simply cannot pick up our lives, our businesses and, even in the absence of "exodus taxes," our wealth and move on to another country. I agree that for frequent international travelers, global business concerns and extremely high net worth individuals that foreign bank accounts may be more a necessity than a luxury, but if you do not fall into one of those categories, you might just be better off having your money in the good ol' U.S. of A.

Investing in Foreign Currencies

Having argued against diversifying into foreign bank accounts, I return, nevertheless, to the original argument that diversifying into foreign currencies is a reasonable investment alternative. There are various ways to accomplish this though investments domiciled in this country. Depending on your individual investment situation, though, it may not be practical to have the actual cash or bonds in foreign currencies. For example, the minimums for foreign bond denominations is typically $10,000 or higher.

All is not lost, however, even for the more modest investor. If you invest in a foreign stock or a country-(or regional-) specific mutual fund, you are actually investing simultaneously in that country's currency (or the entire region's currencies). Although the American Depository Receipt (ADR) of that stock or the mutual fund will not be listed in terms of the foreign currency, the underlying currency value will be reflected in the dollar price of the stock or net asset value of the fund. This is a good reason to stay abreast of currency values. Watch the direction of your stock or mutual fund compared with the direction of the underlying currency.

Morgan Stanley has created an interesting instrument called WEBS listed on the American Stock Exchange. WEBS stand for World Equity Benchmark Shares. In early 2000 there were 17 different WEBS with each one tracking the performance of a specified foreign stock index. These instruments trade just as normal stocks do and provide an interesting currency play of the country involved. However, note that ADRs, country specific country funds or WEBS do not offer a pure currency play. Their value can also vary with the performance of the individual foreign companies or the country's stock index.

Another way for the investor of modest wealth to diversify into foreign currencies is through a global or regional foreign-bond mutual fund. You should be aware, however, that the value of bonds and the value of the underlying currency will frequently move in opposite directions. This happens because the value of bonds is inversely related to the interest rate. As interest rates drop, the asset value of the bonds will increase. On the other hand, as interest rates drop the financial community perceives this as inflationary, so the value of the currency compared to the U.S. dollar or a basket of currencies decreases. The net result is that your return is often no better than the average coupon rates of the bonds owned by the mutual fund. In no case, however, should you view these investments as merely a vehicle for a good rate of return. Beside interest rates, other factors ranging from strikes to elections to wars can influence the value of a country's currency. Thus it is a good idea to keep an eye on both the net asset value of the fund as well as on the currencies.

What I'm suggesting in the last two paragraphs may seem like a lot of trouble just for a little extra diversification. First, let me dispel the notion that it's a lot of trouble. If you are already getting *The Wall Street Journal,* for example, go to the **Money and Investing** section, and while you're looking up the prices of your stocks or mutual funds anyway, go to the page with the topic headings CURRENCY TRADING and FOREIGN EXCHANGE. Under CURRENCY TRADING take a few seconds to check the dollar values of currencies you are interested in, then under FOREIGN EXCHANGE take a minute or two to read the latest news on currency directions. After you form a habit of doing this, I believe you will find it fascinating, and you may even miss doing so those few days of the year that you are away for a holiday or on vacation. You will find that G-7 agreements, Central Bank movements and import/export considerations can affect short-term currency values. Still, the longer-term direction of a nation's currency will give a good indication of the underlying economic strength of that country.

In the remainder of this chapter I will point out specific foreign currency investment opportunities that I believe are highly attractive, though not necessarily appropriate for everyone. Addresses and tele-phone numbers are provided so you may investigate further.

everbank.com World Markets

everbank.com in St. Louis, Missouri offers two foreign currency accounts. These are:

1. WorldCurrency Access™ Accounts—these are basically deposit accounts with interest rates tiered to reflect the size of the deposit. Though no minimum deposits are required, there are minimum deposits required to earn interest Examples of these minimums in early 2000 range from 6,501 British Pounds Sterling to 9,000 euros to 1,000,001 Japanese Yen. These accounts should be used mainly to hedge the U.S. dollar which is also one of the currency accounts available. Your money can be held in this dollar account whenever the dollar is showing exceptional strength.

2. WorldCurrency™ Certificates of Deposit—these certificates are deposits of everbank.com in foreign currencies with rates of interest indicative of rates paid in the foreign country for deposits of similar size. The minimum investment in these CDs is the equivalent of $20,000.

Note that for either of these investment options, investors receive F.D.I.C. protection, though this protection does not extend to losses due to currency fluctuations. everbank.com charges no direct fees on these transactions but I note that the spread (ask and bid) on the currency values is not insignificant, so frequent trading is not recommended.

To obtain additional information and application forms, you can contact everbank.com as follows:

everbank.com
everbank World Markets
555 North New Dallas Road
Suite 110
St. Louis, MO 63141
(800)-926-4922

Ask to speak to David Ott, who will give you excellent service. David Ott is also the editor of *Review & Focus*, an excellent newsletter on the currency markets.

For most currency investors reading this book, I would recommend the WorldCurrency Access™ Account. As I mentioned above, use it to hedge the U.S. dollar. Find a foreign currency you like, perhaps one that is just starting to gain against the U.S. dollar. Look for major long-term trends (1-5 years) and do not trade on minor changes in the currency value. Don't worry about missing the exact high or low for the currency against the dollar. Remember, if the dollar is looking strong, you can always park your cash in a U.S. dollar account, until you feel certain that trend reverses. As an example, in 1993 the Swiss franc hit an intermediate term low of about 65¢ against the dollar. By early 1996 it reached nearly 90¢. Even if you missed the low and high and, say, got in at 68¢ and back out at 85¢ you would have made $2,500 on a $10,000 investment or a 25% return (17¢ divided by 68¢) in a little over two years. That's not bad for having your money in cash. Since the beginning of 1996 the Swiss franc has declined from nearly 90¢ to about 60¢ in early 2000. The Swiss franc at 60¢ offers good value for currency investors and bears watching for any breakout to the upside from this level.

The Pioneer Vision Variable Annuity

Another foreign currency investment opportunity involves retirement assets. This is the first U.S. variable annuity with a fund denominated in Swiss francs. This fund was developed in conjunction with Pioneer Vision Variable Annuity which, in turn, is issued by Allmerica Financial Life Insurance and Annuity Company (First Allmerica Financial Life in New York and Hawaii). The Swiss Franc Bond Portfolio offered by Pioneer is made up of high-quality, short to intermediate term Swiss franc denominated bonds. The fund aims to approximate the performance of the Swiss franc relative to the dollar while earning a reasonable level of income.

The beauty of investing in the Pioneer Vision Variable Annuity, in my opinion, is twofold. First, the Swiss Franc Bond Portfolio is one of fourteen portfolios (as of this writing) where you can park your money, including a fixed principle Money Market Portfolio. Thus, if the Swiss franc is undergoing a bit of a retrenchment, as it has during the past several years, you can switch your money into one of these other funds. There are up to 12 free transfers allowed per year. As I mentioned above, don't switch around on every tiny movement of the Swiss franc, and don't worry about hitting its top and bottoms in value against the dollar. If you are following the currency, maybe even doing some charting, and keeping abreast of the overall currency markets (i.e., noting whether the dollar is currently hot or not), you will be able to discern the longer term direction.

Second, the assets of a variable annuity are segregated from the assets of the servicing insurance company. In fact, the assets of each portfolio are segregated. That means that the value of the contract is dependent on the assets of the underlying investments and not on the overall financial condition of the insurer. Even though Allmerica is a highly rated company, I find this feature of the variable annuity very attractive. You should note that fixed annuity contracts do not share his feature of having their assets segregated from the assets of the insurer.

There are a number of other attractive features of the Pioneer Vision Variable Annuity. There include:

* Tax deferral on your investment earnings until withdrawal
* Guaranteed death benefit—the greatest of the total amount contributed, the total account value, or the highest account value on any fifth-year policy anniversary, plus subsequent payments
* Minimum investments—$600 minimum initial investment ($1000 in Washington state), $50 minimum subsequent investment
* IRA option
* No initial sales charges, $30 annual fee which is waived for account values over $50,000, no withdrawal charges on amounts invested for more than seven years
* Avoid the 1% excise tax on offshore annuities

You will need a broker/representative to open an account. Not everyone handles these annuities. A broker who does is George W. Doerner who can be reached at:

J.J.B. Hilliard, W.L. Lyons, Inc.
9 Pack Square, SW, Suite 300
Asheville, NC 28801
(877)-538-7698

Lintz Glover/Mark Twain

If you would like to open an investment account that would enable you to buy, hold and sell currency cash deposits, stocks and bonds from any country in the world, you may wish to contact Neil J. George, Jr. at Lintz Glover/Mark Twain. Mr. George is an international economist and is widely recognized as an expert in international investing. He is the editor of *World Brief*—also know as "The Pink" because of the paper it is printed on—a newsletter detailing the international markets. Lintz Glover/Mark Twain allows you to open a variety of accounts, ranging from personal to trust accounts to IRAs to managed accounts and Internet accounts. Incidentally, the company has an excellent website at www.lintz.net. You can reach Neil J. George, Jr. at:

Lintz Glover/Mark Twain
Global Markets
15260 Ventura Boulevard
Suite 1110
Sherman Oaks, CA 91403
(800)-959-2397

Miles Franklin, Ltd.

You can also invest directly in a Swiss franc annuity offered by a Swiss insurance company. Foreign annuities do not have the reporting requirements of a foreign bank account, but the minimum to start an annuity can be $10,000 US or more. Companies exist to facilitate the purchase of Swiss annuities. One such company is BFI Consulting AG. One of their US contacts is Miles Franklin, Ltd., mentioned in Chapter 7. Contact either Bob Sichel or Andy Schectman.

Miles Franklin, Ltd.
3601 Park Center Building, #306
St. Louis Park, MN 55416
(800)-822-8080

In conclusion, I think you can see that there are many possibilities of diversifying outside the U.S. dollar without having to open a foreign bank account. Keep your investing eye on a basket of currencies, and I believe it will improve your overall awareness and enjoyment of investing.

References

1. David Ott, Editor, *Review and Focus*, everbank.com, St. Louis, MO (A newsletter on foreign exchange and international markets.)

2. Neil J. George, Jr., *World Brief*, Linz Glover/Mark Twain, Sherman Oaks, CA (A newsletter on international markets)

Chapter 9

Exotics

Take calculated risks. That is quite different from being rash.

General George Smith Patton

A Primer on Futures

This chapter is about futures contracts and the options on those futures contacts. I know, I know…. You're thinking that I'm going to try to talk you into throwing your hard earned money away in the risky, volatile world of the Chicago and New York futures pits. Quite the contrary. I advise that you do *not* speculate in the futures market. It is estimated that anywhere from 90-97% of all participants trading in the futures markets lose money. However, the futures markets are so huge in terms of the volume of daily turnover and so important to the institutions that deal in the underlying commodities or financials that I think it is a terrible mistake to ignore these markets entirely.

It is not at all difficult to follow these markets—read on and I will try to get you through some of the gobbledygook—if you subscribe to either *The Wall Street Journal* or *Investor's Business Daily*. Even in these respected newspapers, however, limited coverage is afforded to the commodities markets, but at least these papers list the contract prices every trading day. Furthermore, it is clear that even some seemingly unrelated markets are in fact interrelated, so it is prudent to know if something unusual (i.e., price spikes or drops) is happening in any particular area.

You could argue that you can keep current by merely watching the spot prices of commodities plus the stock and bond prices, but every market is discounted for what will happen six to twelve months down the road, and the futures markets give you the best estimate of what future prices will be.

For example, if you own or plan to buy stock shares in a company dealing in a particular commodity, you might want to follow the corresponding commodity as outlined in Table 9-1.

So just what are these futures contracts, anyway, and how do they work? First allow me to give you an example that I made up all by myself and that I like and which didn't seem so funny one Halloween season when I had a difficult time finding a pumpkin for my little boy after the first one we had went bad. Pumpkins? No, as far as I know there are no futures contracts on pumpkins, but if you follow this example you'll see how we could set up such a contract and in the process learn just about everything on the basics of futures. Suppose one sunny day in mid-July you are driving in the countryside and spot a field of ripening pumpkins. This reminds you that the previous year you were almost unable to get a second pumpkin for your little boy as Halloween was fast approaching. You stop and negotiate with the farmer to buy two pumpkins one week before Halloween, October 24. This is the "delivery date" of the commodity, in this case pumpkins.

Industry	Commodity
food, agricultural (depending on business)	wheat, corn, oats, soybeans, orange juice cattle, hogs, sugar, coffee, cocoa
paper, construction	lumber
mining (depending on business)	copper, precious metals, nickel, aluminum, lead
energy	crude oil, heating oil, unleaded gas, natural gas
textiles	cotton
banking, brokerage	bonds, notes, t-bills, eurodollars
exporters	currencies

Table 9-1

You and the farmer agree on a price of $2.50 per pumpkin. This is 5 to 10 cents more that what pumpkins are presently selling for but you agree because the farmer in the meantime has overhead, for example insurance costs and storage expense, before the delivery date. These expenses are referred to as "carrying charges." Notice that there are two participants in this and in every futures contract agreement. You, as the buyer, are said to be "long" two pumpkins, while the farmer, as the seller, is said to be "short" two pumpkins. You have agreed to take delivery of two pumpkins on October 24 for $2.50 per pumpkin, and he has agreed to deliver two pumpkins on the same date for the same price.

As a good faith gesture, you agree to put up a quarter (or 10% of the purchase price in this case) for each pumpkin, your "margin" on the contract, and the farmer, as a gesture of good faith that he will deliver the pumpkins, agrees to put up a quarter on each pumpkin, his margin on the contract. The worker who drives the farmer's tractor agrees to hold the money and so acts as the "broker" in this transaction. For doing this he requests a nickel from each of us for each pumpkin. This is his "commission."

There are several issues to note at this point. As mentioned above both the buyer and seller put up margin money equal in this case to 10% of the purchase price. That means that both parties are highly leveraged on this transaction (to be precise, both are 90% leveraged).

This leverage will not be an important factor unless between mid-July and October 24 the price of pumpkins varies substantially from its original purchase price. Note also that the nickel per pumpkin commission is only 2% of the total purchase price of $2.50, but the broker handles only the margin money, not the entire purchase price. Thus, his commission is 20% of your margin—these percentages are quite typical in the futures industry. The margin money is not spent and gone forever. You get it back plus your gain or minus your loss on the transaction when you terminate (sell) your contract.

You drive back home, feeling contented with your transaction, secure in the knowledge that two pumpkins will be waiting for you on October 24. However, by the end of July and into the beginning of August, there are several rainy days and many hot, humid days which all combine to lead everyone, from your neighbor to the local grocery store manager, to believe that there will be a bumper crop of pumpkins this year. "Indeed," the grocery store manager boasts, "the 'supply' of pumpkins this year should be excellent." In fact, the crop looks so good that the tractor driver who acted as your broker calls to tell you that the price of pumpkins has dropped to $2.35. The drop in price isn't too severe just yet, but he informs you that if the price does drop further he may have to ask you to put up more money (a "margin call") just to make sure you carry out your end of the deal. Obviously, if you felt the price of pumpkins were going much lower, it would be prudent to sell your contract to your neighbor or someone else for $2.35 (i.e., "offset" your position) and pay the farmer the difference to get out of your contract for $2.50.

However, you still feel confident that $2.50 is a good price for your pumpkins, so you keep your contract. By the middle of August news leaks out that vine borers have taken a firm hold in the surrounding area and suddenly the cucumber, squash, and pumpkin crops look to be in danger. The price of pumpkins jumps to $3.00 and you look like a genius because if you take delivery you will have saved 45 cents (50¢ minus the 5¢ commission) on each pumpkin.

The end of August brings more bad news for pumpkins (but good news for you). Since there hasn't been any rain all month long, it seems the later developing pumpkins will never be ready by Halloween and hence not for your delivery date. Pumpkin prices soar to $3.50.

The farmer who sold you your contact and who has been short the pumpkin market during the sharp rise in prices (and who has by now endured two margin calls) sees more bad news ahead. He finally throws in the towel and offsets his contract by agreeing to pay his farming neighbor $1.00 per pumpkin if farmer #2 will agree to deliver the two pumpkins to you on October 24. You don't care who delivers the pumpkins as long as your little boy gets his jack-o-lantern.

Farmer #1, the original seller, showed great wisdom in offsetting his contract, because by mid-September it is clear that a blight will further reduce the supply of pumpkins. Pumpkins soar to the unheard of price of $4.25.

Your neighbor, who also has a little boy, is getting very nervous by this time, and after you let it drop that you have this arrangement with farmer #2, he talks you into selling one of your pumpkin contracts to him for $1.75. In the process you effectively offset one of your contacts and indeed take profits on your original margin of 25¢ of 680% ($1.75 profit on the contract minus 5¢ divided by 25¢). Could pumpkin speculation really be this easy?

The pumpkin bull market continues into October as it is revealed that all the local schools will be engaging in a jack-o-lantern contest (the demand side of the equation). Pumpkin prices skyrocket to $5.00.

You, however, feel very smug knowing you will receive your pumpkin for $2.50, because on October 1 you acknowledged that you would indeed be taking delivery of the commodity on your remaining contract from farmer #2. The day on which you must declare whether you will be taking delivery of your commodity is called the "first notice date."

Finally on October 24, you take delivery of your pumpkin and save $2.50 on the going price, in effect making a profit of $2.45 (the difference between $5.00 and $2.50 minus your 5¢ commission) for an overall return of 980%. Even your neighbor, who got into the pumpkin market at $4.25 (clearly a trend follower or momentum player, not a long term investor like yourself) saved 75¢, in effect making a profit of 70¢ and a return of 280% assuming that his margin was also 25¢. As prices and price volatility of commodities increase, the exchanges often raise the margin requirements, sometimes dramatically.

It should be clear, even from this simple example, that the allure of these kinds of returns are addictive. Not everyone prospered in these transactions, however. Farmer #1, the man you originally brought your pumpkin contracts from, lost $1.05 per pumpkin ($3.50 minus $2.50 minus his 5¢ commission). His net return was a negative 420% (ouch!). Farmer #2 did even worse. He received $3.45 for his pumpkin ($1.00 from farmer #1 and $2.50 from you minus his 5¢ commission) but could have received $5.00 on the spot market on October 24, in effect losing $1.55 on the transaction with a negative return of 620% assuming his margin was also 25¢ (double ouch!!).

It is said the futures/commodities markets is a "zero sum game." This is because there are always two participants in any transaction. One is a buyer or "long" the market, the other is a seller or "short" the market. Neither can gain without the other losing. In actuality, as Dr. Alexander Elder points out in his fascinating book, *Trading for a Living*, and which you may have already recognized from the above example, the situation is worse than that—it is a "minus sum game." There is a third party, the broker, who siphons off funds no matter who wins or loses. Just considering commissions alone, even if pumpkin prices would have remained at $2.50 throughout the growing season and into Halloween, each participant would have effectively lost 5¢ (to commissions) for a net return of a negative 20% on the margin deposit. Of course, each participant would have achieved his objective—you ensured that you would receive your pumpkins and farmer #1 ensured that he would be able to sell his pumpkins. This was the original intention of the futures market. In a capitalist system, however, somebody will always figure out ways to make (or lose) money. Today it is estimated that nearly 97% of all futures contract are offset (canceled—see above example) before delivery. This would seem to imply that a lot of speculation goes on in the futures markets.

The example of the pumpkin futures contact is not that farfetched. If we increased the number of pumpkins per contract to 5000, then at $2-$3 per pumpkin the total value of each contract would be in the $10,000 to $15,000 range, not at all unreasonable. A move of each cent in the pumpkin price would correspond to a $50 gain or loss per contract. We might impose the restriction that prices on our contract could move no more than 12¢ in either direction on a given day based on the previous day's close. This is referred to as a "limit move." Trading in the contract would stop when the limit was reached. Our contract (delivery) dates might be a more reasonable second Friday each October, November and December (the latter two coinciding with the pumpkin pie eating season at Thanksgiving and Christmas). In addition, delivery points might be set up at various locations around the country. The contract at this point would be "standardized" so that any farmer, pie-maker, pumpkin speculator or jack-o-lantern freak could buy or sell without knowing, or caring, who he was dealing with.

The grain contracts on the Chicago Board of Trade (CBOT) are based on 5000 bushels. Each 1¢ move in the wheat, corn, oats or soybean price means a $50 move in their respective contracts. And corn over the past twenty years has, except for very brief periods, been priced somewhere between $2-3. Substitute a bushel of corn for a pumpkin in our above example and little would change. The daily limit move for corn is 12¢. The contacts months for corn (as well as for wheat and oats) are March, May, July, September and December.

The contact sizes for other commodities can be slightly unusual. For example, the contract size for coffee is 37,500 pounds, making a 1¢/lb. move in its contract worth $375. In contrast, the contract size for gold is a mere 100 troy ounces. Still, a $1/oz move in gold is worth $100. Contract sizes are listed along with the daily futures prices in the newspapers mentioned above. In general, the equivalent unit moves in contract price are easy to figure out.

In very similar fashion it is possible to create futures contacts based on financial instruments. You merely designate a given quantity of currency as the contract size (e.g., 125,000 Swiss francs), value it against the U.S. dollar, and presto you have a foreign currency future. A 1¢ move in the Swiss franc changes the value of the contract by $1,250. Similarly, treasury bonds and notes, t-bills and eurodollars, as well as other debt obligations, can be so bundled. To get futures on indices you can, for example, define one point on the S&P 500 to be equal to $500. By default, the contract size is then $500 times the value of S&P 500 Index. You can extend this abstraction to such things as bundling particle emission (pollution control) allowances from smokestacks and to electricity sold across state borders.

The types of traders in the futures markets are classified into three broad groups. The "commercials" are traders whose businesses actually buy or sell the underlying commodities and who use futures as a hedge against adverse price moves. The other two groups are the "large speculators," primarily commodity funds, and the "small speculators," primarily the public. The commercials and large speculators are considered the "smart money," while the small speculators are for the most part considered clueless.

This brief introduction to the futures markets is intended neither to be comprehensive nor is it meant to coax you into becoming a wild-eyed speculator in commodities. There is still much I haven't told you, like getting stuck in a series of limit up or limit down days without being able to offset your (most likely losing) contract. On the other hand, I hope the above discussion shows you that you don't have to be afraid of the futures markets, especially if you are merely following them and are not risking your hard-earned money. I probably follow the futures markets more closely than I do the stock markets (perhaps to my investing detriment) although I have much more money at risk in stocks. I think if you start following the futures markets, which only takes a few more minutes per day of your time, you will find them both interesting and rewarding.

Options on Futures Contracts

Before I close this chapter, I want to briefly discuss options on futures. While many financial pundits consider futures contracts as "derivatives," I do not. Options of any kind, however, are true derivatives. However, compared to the way various financial instruments can be bundled nowadays, then torn apart and rebundled, both stock options and options on futures are very primitive derivatives.

The owner of a futures option has the right, but not the obligation, to buy or sell the underlying commodity at a given price (the "strike price") until a certain date, at which time that right expires. An option is said to possess "intrinsic value" (depending on how close in price the underlying commodity is to the strike price) and "time value" (demanding a higher premium the farther away the expiration date). An option is a "wasting asset" in that if it is not resold or exercised in a timely fashion, it expires worthless.

The owner of a "call" option has the right to buy at the strike price (before a certain date) and is "long" the market. He pays a one time premium (plus commission) for that right. The person who sold him the call option is "short" the market. If the price of the underlying commodity is above the strike price, the option is said to be "in the money," and the owner is happy. If the price is below the strike price, the option is said to be "out of the money," and the owner is sad. If the price is equal to the strike price, the option is said to be "at the money," and the owner is anxious.

As an example, in early 2000 a May 2000 crude oil call option with a $30/barrel strike price listed for around $1. Since crude oil futures contracts are based on 1000 barrels, this option would have cost you $1000. This purchase would, in effect, put you long 1000 barrels of crude oil. If crude oil for delivery in May 2000 would trade at $35, your option would be worth at least $5 ($35-$30 strike price) and you could sell your option for a profit of $4000. However, if crude oil trades at less than $30/barrel by the expiration date, your option could expire worthless. You would have no further obligation.

The call option would give you the right to buy a futures contract at $30/barrel. Rarely would you exercise the option, but rather you would sell your position to another buyer to realize your gain. Most options expire prior to the corresponding futures contract, usually by a month to six weeks.

The owner of a "put" option has the right to sell at a certain price (before a certain date) and is "short" the market. He pays a one time premium (plus commission) for that right. The person who sold him that option is "long" the market. In the case of a put, if the price of the underlying commodity is above the strike price, the option is said to be "out of the money," just the opposite of the call option. If the price is below the strike price, the put option is "in the money."

Just as in the case of futures contracts, option contracts are standardized, so you don't know (and don't care) who you are buying from or selling to. The leverage in options can be tremendous and very tempting. Just remember that those guys in Chicago and New York are no dummies and they generally have the premiums figured out to be more than commensurate to the risk involved.

In summary,

contract	commission	premium	consequences
long futures	yes	margin deposit	obligation to accept delivery
short futures	yes	margin deposit	obligation to deliver
long call option	yes	pay premium	right to buy commodity at strike price by specified date
short call option	yes	receive premium	obligation to sell at strike price if call exercised by specified date
long put option	yes	pay premium	right to sell at strike price until specified date
short put option	yes	receive premium	obligation to buy at strike price if put exercised by specified date.

Table 9-2

References

1. Ginger Szala, Editor, *Futures Magazine*, Oster Communications, Cedar Falls, Iowa (monthly news magazine; for subscription call 800-635-3931; www.futuresmag.com).

2. Jack D. Schwager, *A Complete Guide to the Futures Markets*, John Wiley & Sons, New York, NY, 1984.

3. *Options on Agricultural Futures*, Chicago Board of Trade, Chicago, IL, 1989.

Chapter 10

Who Is This Guy Fibonacci Anyway?

...Fibonacci's only monuments are a statue across the Arno River from the Leaning Tower and two streets which bear his name.... It seems strange that so few visitors to the 179-foot marble Tower of Pisa, which leans seventeen feet out from the perpendicular, have ever heard of Fibonacci or seen his statue.

A. J. Frost and Robert R. Prechter, Jr. in *Elliott Wave Principle*

Leonardo Fibonacci da Pisa was an Italian mathematician who lived in the twelfth and thirteenth centuries. He is credited with discovering or rediscovering the following infinite mathematical series:

1, 1, 2, 3, 5, 8, 13, 21, 34, 55, 89, 144, 233,....

This series has the interesting property that beginning with 1, 1 every number thereafter is the sum of the preceding two numbers in the sequence (i.e., 1+1=2, 1+2=3, 2+3=5, 3+5=8, and so on). A second interesting property is that the ratio of any two adjacent numbers in the sequence oscillates around the irrational number 1.61803..., getting closer and closer as the numbers increase in size. This irrational number, often rounded to 1.618, is called the Golden Ratio or Golden Mean, and is sometimes designated by the capital Greek letter *psi*, Φ. The inverse of Φ is another irrational number 0.61803..., usually rounded to 0.618. The difference between Φ and its inverse is one, i.e., 1.618-0.618 = 1. Also note that 1-0.618 = 0.382 and 0.618 x 0.618 = 0.382.

There are a number of other interesting properties of the Fibonacci series, but I refer you to the references for these. The reason for introducing this subject here is that is has been observed that in many instances financial markets retrace their upward movements by approximately the percentages given by the Fibonacci ratios. For example, if a heavily owned stock moves from one level to another, say from a price of $30 to $40, then when is corrects you might expect it to fall 0.382 x ($10 move up) = $3.82, or approximately 3 13/16 points to 36 3/16. Another possibility is a fall of 0.618 x ($10 move up) = $6.18, or approximately 6 3/16 points to 33 13/16. When a stock or market falls back in price in this manner, these pullbacks are known as **retracements**, and depending upon other factors can represent excellent buying opportunities. Another common retracement is 50%, but this, too, can be argued to be a Fibonacci ratio, namely 1/2.

The Fibonacci series and ratios are manifested throughout nature and are important in many fields ranging from art and music to architecture and engineering. It has been suggested that these ratios come into play in the financial markets because mass psychology governs the markets and mass psychology is just another natural phenomenon. I will allow others to defend this position. I merely note that other retracement ratios, besides the ones mentioned above, are observed in the financial markets. However, there are enough Fibonacci ratios and numbers obtained by subtracting these ratios from the digit one to cover almost any situation. Nevertheless, retracements of 38%, 50% and 62% occur frequently enough to warrant our attention.

The use of such ratios in evaluating stocks and financial markets is an example of technical analysis, the real subject of this chapter. In brief,

technical analysis is the study of price charts of the financial markets with the goal of predicting future prices. This is an overly simple definition, but it is sufficient for our purposes. A pure technical analyst would argue that he can derive everything he needs to know about a given market from its price chart. The study of supply and demand factors, company earnings, future prospects and so on is known as fundamental analysis. Some investors are concerned only with fundamentals. However, most professional investors in today's markets use both fundamental and technical analysis, and it is my opinion that even the beginning investor should have at least a rudimentary knowledge of these subjects as well.

In the remainder of this chapter I will introduce you to some basic concepts in technical analysis, such as trendlines, support and resistance, moving averages and different ways to chart prices. Though most technical analysis these days is done by computer, trendlines and support and resistance lines can be drawn easily with a pencil and ruler.

In this guide I can barely scratch the surface of this still developing field. If I am successful in piquing your interest I hope you will investigate some of the excellent references at the end of the chapter.

Trendlines

Financial markets do not move in straight lines but rather in a series of zigzags. These zigzags can resemble saw-teeth or more commonly a series of water waves, either pattern displaying alternating peaks and troughs. An **uptrend** is price action where successive peaks and troughs are advancing. A **downtrend** is price action where successive peaks and troughs are declining. A **sideways trend** is price action where successive peaks and troughs are approximately horizontal.

Trendlines are straight lines that indicate the direction of price on a chart. An **up trendline** is a straight line drawn in an uptrend from the lowest trough up along successive troughs. In Figure 10-1 an up trendline (up TL) is shown for a monthly chart of Raytheon Co., a large defense contractor. Note the price repeatedly bounces up away from the trendline. If you can identify a valid trendline in an up move, you should be prepared to buy when the price moves back to the trendline. If the price moves through the trendline, then the trendline is said to be broken, or **violated**. This happens in dramatic fashion at the far right in Figure 10-1.

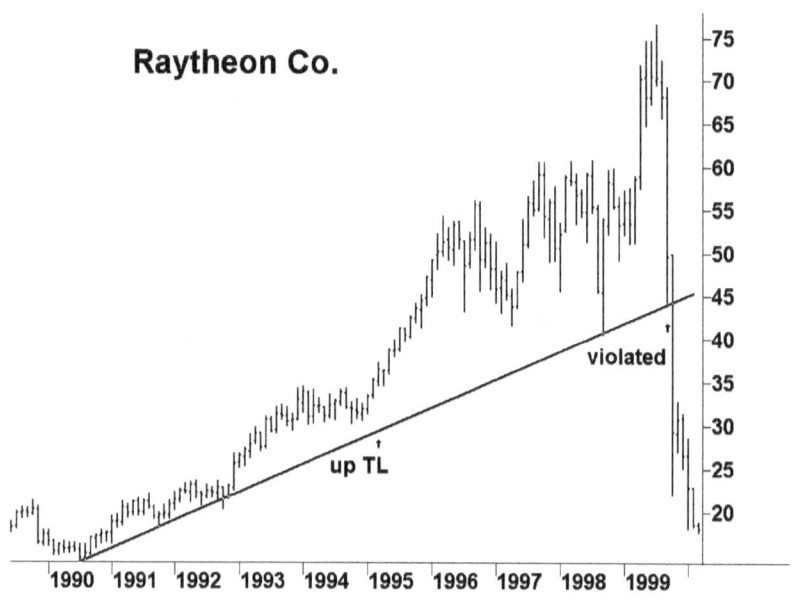

Fig. 10-1

A **down trendline** is a straight line drawn in a downtrend from the highest peak down along successive peaks. In Figure 10-2 a down trendline is shown for the spot price of platinum. Note that the price repeatedly knocks up against the trendline. If you can identify a valid trendline in a down move, you should be prepared to sell when the price moves back to the trendline. Once the trendline was violated in Figure 10-2 at about $380/ounce, an uptrend to well over $500/ounce followed.

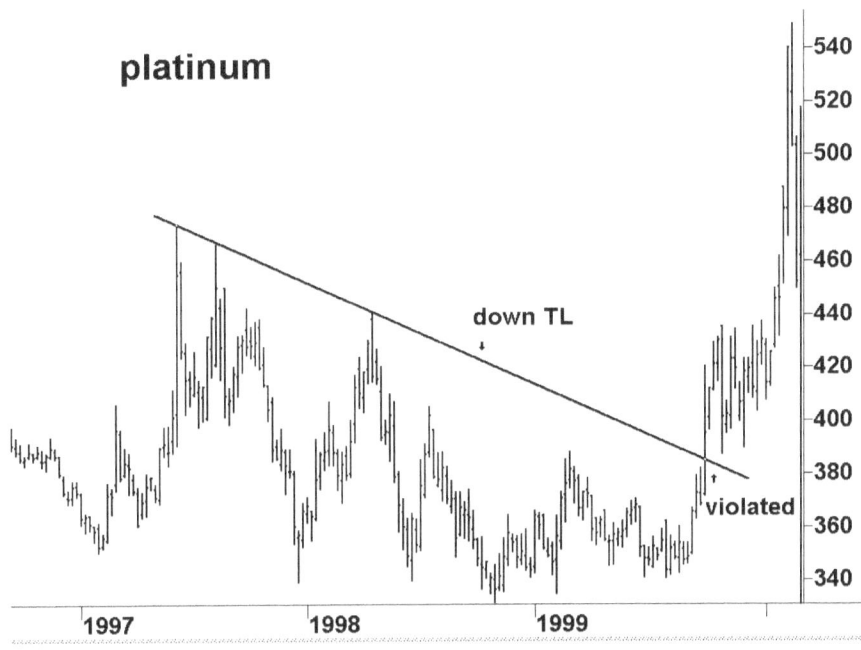

Fig. 10-2

For a sideways trend the concept of trendlines is less useful than that of **channel lines**. In this case the two channel lines are merely horizontal straight lines, one connecting successive peaks and another connecting successive troughs. An example is given by Coca Cola during 1992-94 (see Figure 10-3). If price breaks out of a channel significantly in either direction a strong move in that direction usually follows.

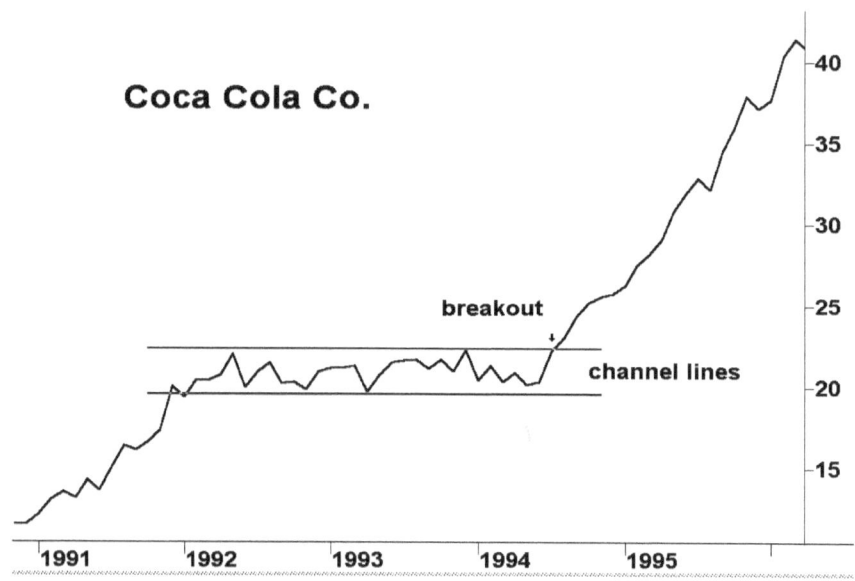

Fig. 10-3

Support and Resistance

Support is a price level where buyers (bulls) have a stronger hand than sellers (bears). Another way of saying this is that support is a price level where buying interest is strong enough to overcome any selling pressure. Support is most often represented on charts by troughs. But when prices bounce away from an up trendline, the trendline can be said to be a level of support. Also prices will sometimes decline until they meet a certain average price level. That average price is then said to be a level of support.

Resistance is a price level where sellers have the upper hand over buyers. Another way of saying this is that resistance is a price level where selling pressure overcomes buying interest. Resistance is most often represented on charts by peaks. However, when prices knock up against a down trendline, the trendline can be said to be a level of resistance. Or when prices rise to meet an average price level, that average price level can represent resistance.

An example of support and resistance is given by DaimlerChryster stock, shown in Figure 10-4. After an initial run up in price after the merger of Daimler Benz and Chryster, this stock struggled to maintain its highs. In the latter half of 1999 the price fell to the $65 level. This $65 level subsequently became a level of support. On several attempted rebounds the stock price was unable to break through a resistance level just below $80.

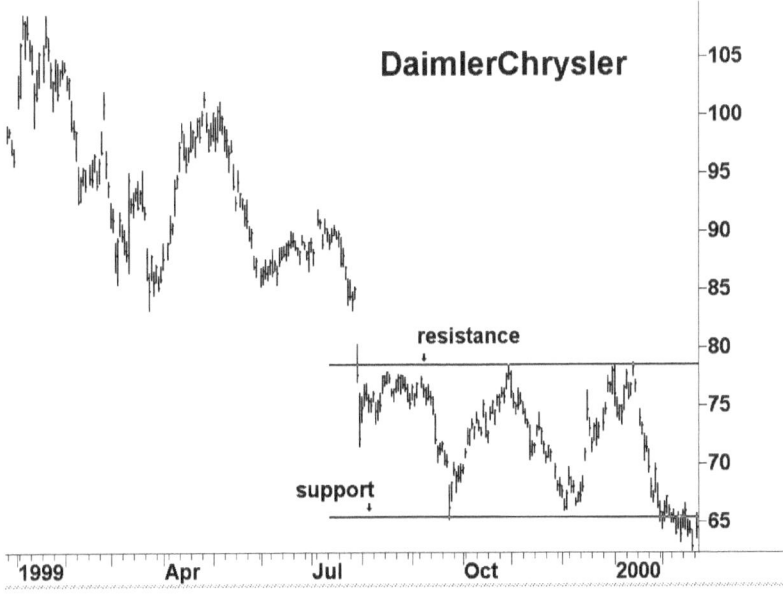

Fig 10-4

All price charts in any financial markets have these levels of support and resistance, and after you gain a modest level of experience you should be able to pick them out visually. As a whole investor you should always be aware of levels of support and resistance for investments you are considering. Levels of support frequently represent excellent buying opportunities. However, if levels of support are violated significantly you should realize this investment choice was not prudent and cut your losses immediately. If the investment begins an up move from a lower level you can always take another flyer on it again later. Levels of resistance often represent excellent selling opportunities or excellent price objectives. If an investment has difficulty breaking through a certain price level after repeated tries, you might be better off taking profits and watching the price action from the sidelines. If the investment declines in price, you can always get back in at a lower level. If the investment finally breaks through a resistance level by a significant amount, here, too, you can jump back on board and ride it to the next resistance level.

These techniques may give the impression that we are jumping into and out of markets too frequently. This need not be the case nor should it be. I recommend looking at daily, weekly and monthly charts for both trendlines and for levels of support and resistance. You will find that there are daily trends within weekly trends and weekly trends within monthly trends. For example, the daily trend may be up, the weekly trend down and the monthly trend up, down or sideways. The same arguments regarding time frames can be made for levels of support and resistance. There may be levels of support and resistance on a a daily chart that appear between levels of support and resistance on a weekly or monthly chart.

When you find trends on daily, weekly and monthly charts all in the same direction, these are the really strong trends. Similarly, if you find levels of support or resistance agreeing on daily, weekly and monthly charts, these are the strong levels of support and resistance. I suggest you do your trading only off of strong trends or strong levels of support and resistance.

I feel the concept of support and resistance is so important that I elaborate on this subject in Appendix 2.

Moving Averages

It is with some hesitation that I introduce the concept of moving averages, because up until now everything that has been introduced throughout this chapter and guide is easily done without a computer. Moving averages are best followed with the aid of a computer. I use a computer extensively for my own investing. If you own a computer, you should, too. If you do not own a computer, do not despair. You can still use moving averages, but they are a little move tedious to calculate.

A simple moving average for N days is calculated by taking the sum of the price levels P_1, P_2...P_N for the last N days divided by N. The formula is:

$$(P_1 + P_2 + ... + P_N)/N$$

The "moving" part comes in when we update the average: we drop off the old price from N+1 days ago, add in the new price and again divide by N.

Moving averages give a broader picture of where a given market has been. If the moving average is below the present day's price, you know the price action has been bullish. If the moving average is above the present day's price you know that some enthusiasm has waned. Another way of saying this is that if the slope of the moving average is up, the price action is bullish; if the slope is down, it is bearish.

Instead of the simple moving average, defined above, most technical analysts use either a weighted or an exponential moving average. The reason is that recent price action is more influential on future price direction than price action that happened long ago. Thus in a weighted or exponential moving average more importance is given to recent prices than to older prices.

In Figure 10-5 is shown a weekly chart of AT&T with a 200-day and a 50-day simple moving average (MA) superimposed. Some traders use the crossover of these averages as a buy-sell indicator. When the 50-day moving average crosses over the 200-day average from below this generates a buy signal; when the 50-day average crosses from above, this generates a sell signal.

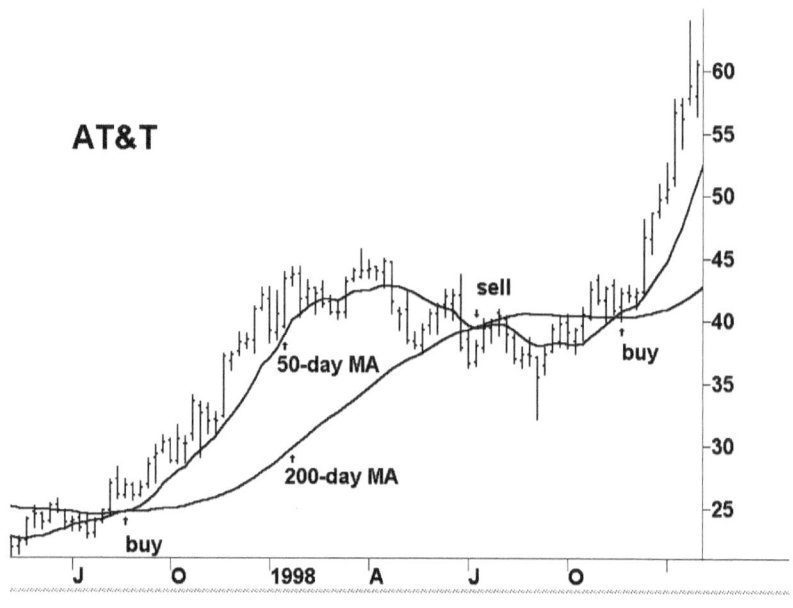

Fig. 10-5

The length of moving average used depends to a great extent on the particular market. For stocks 40, 50, 100 and 200-day moving averages are common. For commodities much shorter periods are used, with 5,

9,10,18 and 20-day moving averages being common. Much testing is done to determine which length of moving average works best with a particular market.

Moving averages are far from the most sophisticated indicators that can be used. With computers it is easy to concoct mathematically complex indicators and to combine them with numerous other indicators. Some of these work better than others and have become fairly popular. Funny things happen on the way to the financial markets, however. It remains true that the good old standbys—trendlines, support and resistance, and moving averages—often work as well, if indeed not better, than the sophisticated indicators.

Different Ways of Looking at Charts

I conclude this very brief introduction to technical analysis by showing different ways that prices can be represented by charts. In the figures presented above I showed either line charts in which the closing prices are connected by a straight line or bar charts in which the price range for a given period is shown by the length of a vertical line. The tick on the left of the bar is the opening price and the tick on the right the closing price for that period. A much older method of charting, but one only more recently widely adopted in this country, is Japanese candlesticks. In Figure 10-6 is shown the exact same daily price chart for Boeing using the three different methods.

Japanese candlesticks are not much different than bar charts, but the visual effect is dramatic. The thick part of a candlestick is called a **real body** and the vertical lines that look like wicks and can stick out of either end are called shadows. The entire length of the candlestick including **shadows** represents the price range for the day. If the real body is white—or more correctly, empty—the opening price is at the bottom of the real body and the closing price is at the top of the real body. In other words a white or empty real body represents a day where the price increased from its opening price. If the real body is black—or more correctly, filled—the opening price is at the top of the real body and the closing price at the bottom of the real body. Thus a black or filled real body represents a day when the price decreased from its opening value.

It is my experience that once you start using candlesticks for your chart analysis, you really don't want to go back to using anything else. I use candlesticks about 95% of the time. There is an entire branch of technical analysis that is devoted to the study to various candlestick patterns. These patterns fall in the general classes of bullish, bearish and continuation (continuation of a trend).

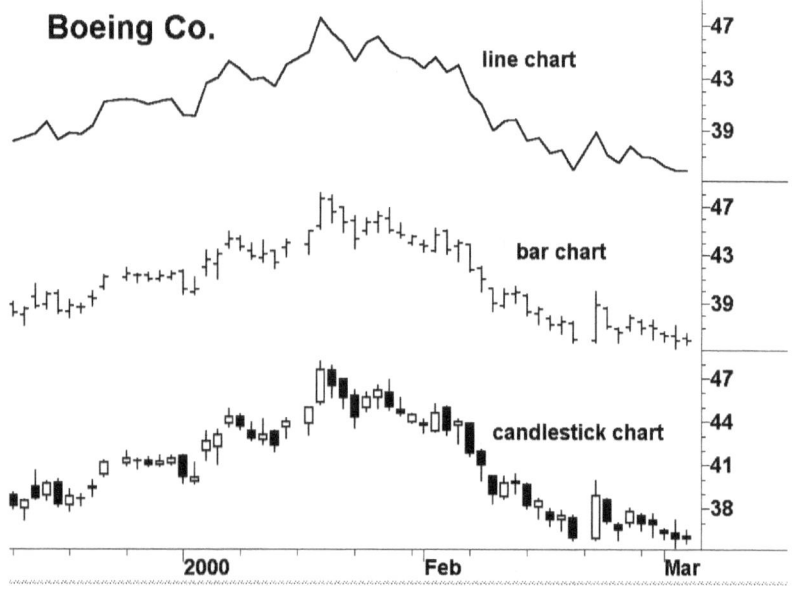

Fig. 10-6

Until now I have only used charts with a linear, or arithmetic, scale for the price axis (vertical axis). However in cases of a rapidly moving market or a long-term trend analysis it is sometimes better to use a logarithmic price scale. On an arithmetic scale each unit price change is represented by an equal distance on the price scale. For example, a price change from 10 to 20 is the same distance as a price change from 90 to 100. On a logarithmic scale the distances on the scale are the same for the same percentage change in price. For example, a price change from 10 to 20 is the same distance as a price change from 50 to 100. In Figure 10-7 is shown a long-term line price chart for the Dow Jones Industrial Average (DJIA) first in arithmetic scale, then in logarithmic scale. The second plot shows that a one thousand-point move in the DJIA isn't what is used to be.

Before concluding this section I want to point out that charts are frequently accompanied by a plot of the trading volume (see Figure 10-8). I haven't given this topic it's due respect in this guide, but consideration of volume is very important in determining the future direction of price action. A one point move in a stock on a high volume of trading can be more important than a three point move on low volume. This is true because the three point move may not be sustainable in the face of increased buying or selling pressure when more traders move into the market. In Figure 8 is shown a daily price chart of Merck, the giant drug company, with the volume of trading underneath. Compare the price action with the volume.

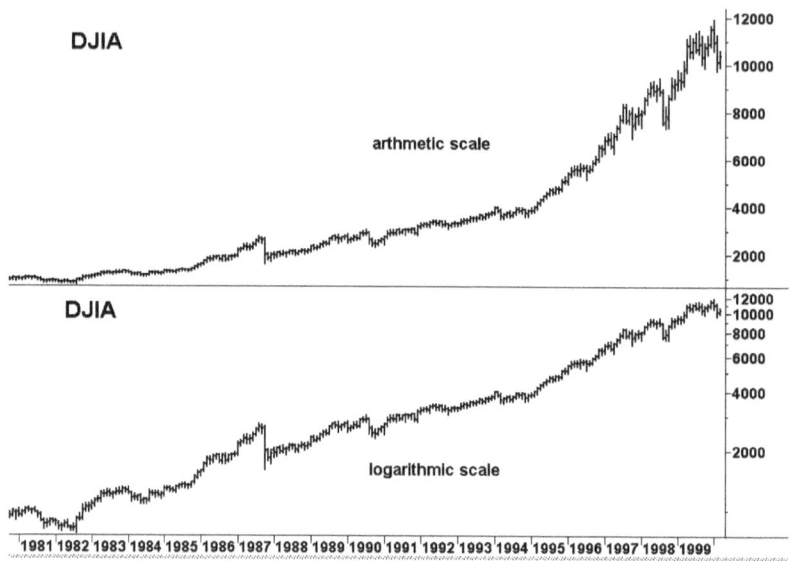

Fig. 10-7

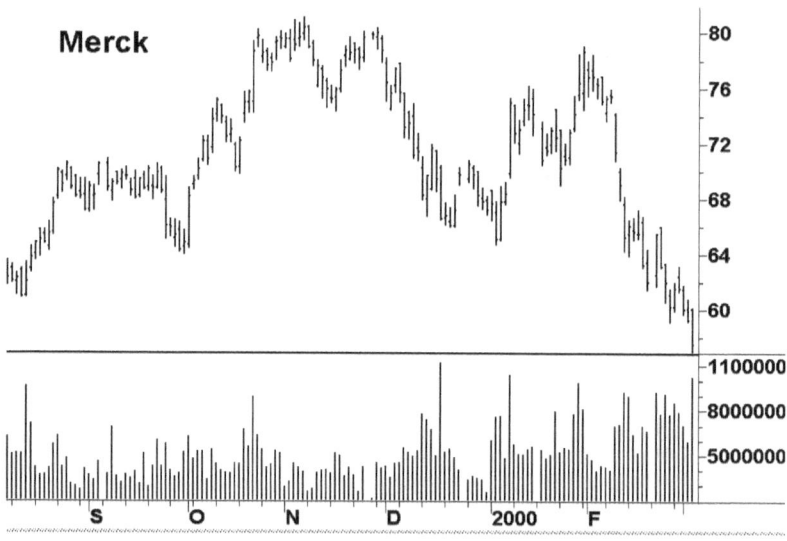

Fig. 10-8

References

1. Dr. Alexander Elder, *Trading for a Living*, John Wiley & Sons, Inc., New York, NY, 1993.

2. John J. Murphy, *Technical Analysis of the Futures Markets*, New York Institute of Finance/Prentice-Hall, New York, NY, 1986. (Don't let the title discourage you—this is one of the best introductions to technical analysis, not just for those interested in the futures market.)

3. John J. Murphy, *Intermarket Technical Analysis*, John Wiley & Sons, Inc, New York, NY, 1991. (Technical analysis applied to the relationship between different markets—an excellent introduction to a topic stressed throughout this guide.)

4. John J. Murphy, *The Visual Investor*, John Wiley & Sons, New York, NY, 1996.

5. Martin J. Pring, *Technical Analysis Explained*, McGraw-Hill, Inc, New York, NY, 1991.

6. Martin J. Pring, *Martin Pring on Market Momentum*, International Institute for Economic Research, Inc., Gloucester, VA, 1993. (Everything you ever wanted to know on moving averages and related topics.)

7. Thomas R. DeMark, *The New Science of Technical Analysis*, John Wiley & Sons, New York, NY, 1994. (Mr. DeMark is considered a technical analysis guru and his book offers new and interesting insights into this field. Note, however, that this book is both somewhat more advanced and more difficult to read, so I highly recommend the beginner start off with Elder, Murphy or Pring.)

8. Louise Yamada, *Market Magic*, John Wiley & Sons, New York, NY, 1998.

9. Tony Plummer, *The Psychology of Technical Analysis*, Probus Publishing Company, Chicago, IL, 1993.

10. Robert Fischer, *Fibonacci Applications and Strategies* for Traders, John Wiley & Sons, Inc., New York, NY, 1993.

11. Steve Nison, *Japanese Candlestick Techniques*, New York Institute of Finance/Simon & Schuster, New York, NY, 1991.

12. Steve Nison, *Beyond Candlesticks*, John Wiley & Sons, New York, NY, 1994.

13. Gregory L. Morris, *CandlePower*, Probus Publishing Company, Chicago, IL, 1992.

14. Thom Hartle, Editor, *Technical Analysis of Stocks & Commodities*, Seattle, WA. (A monthly magazine—for subscription information call 800-832-4642; www.traders.com)

Chapter 11

Market Indices

When the highest type of men hear Tao [the Way],
They diligently practice it.
When the average type of men hear Tao,
They half believe it.
When the lowest type of men hear Tao,
They laugh heartily at it.

Lao-tzu, from *The Way of Loa-tzu*

With the above quote I do not mean to imply that market indices should be compared to the Tao, but I do suggest that only the lowest type of investors sneer at them. Market indices should be considered another important set of tools that can help us interpret markets.

Even novice investors are usually familiar with the broader market indices such as the Dow Jones Industrial Average (DJIA), the S&P 500 index and the Nasdaq composite. However, there are a number of other financial averages that are also important to keep an eye on, if not daily then at least on a weekly basis. These indices can sometimes give clues to the direction of the broader market averages, the direction of inflation and the direction of interest rates. I give a brief introduction below to some of the most well-known and widely watched of these averages.

The Transportation Average

The Dow Jones Transportation Average (DJTA) is a 20 stock index comprised of major airlines, railroads, trucking firms, and general freight companies. Most of the names you would recognize immediately (see the DOW JONES AVERAGES in the *Wall Street Journal*), but you might be surprised to find included Southwest Airlines (LUV—NYSE) or five NASDAQ stocks, including Roadway Express (ROAD) and Yellow Corp. (YELL). Less surprising is the inclusion of FDX Corp. (FDX—NYSE), the holding company of Federal Express, but UPS, which only went public in 1999, was not yet in the Average at the start of the new millennium.

The index has an interesting history. In the July 3, 1884 issue of the *Wall Street Journal* Charles H. Dow first published his stock market average which comprised 11 stocks, nine being those of railroad companies. In 1887 the average was split into two, the Industrial Average containing 12 major industrial stocks and the Rail Average containing 20 major railroad stocks. Over the years as trucking and air travel became important, companies from these areas were included in the Rail Average, and the index name was changed to the Transportation Average.

The DJTA is important for another reason, namely that it is a key element of the so-called "Dow Theory," the granddaddy of modern-day technical analysis. A thorough description of this theory can be found in most books dealing with technical analysis. I only note here that the Dow Theory concerns itself with the direction of the primary market trend, not the duration or size of the trend. In brief, that part of the theory dealing with the DJTA states that the DJIA and the DJTA must confirm one another in order that a clear signal on market trend be given. In other words, according to Dow Theory, a bull market is not confirmed until *both* averages exceed a previous secondary peak. A bear market is not confirmed until *both* averages fall below previous secondary troughs. The two averages do not have to give signals on the same day or the same week, but the closer together they are the stronger the confirmation. At various times during the great bull market of the 1990s the DJIA and the DJTA were both reaching new *all-time* highs simultaneously.

This need for confirmation makes sense from the standpoint that if manufacturing demand is high, then the need to transport raw materials and finished goods should also be high. Hence both sectors should prosper together. If manufacturing demand slackens, then the transport of raw materials and goods should also slow. Some would argue that in contrast to the old manufacturing economy, where the transportation sector was vital, transports have little to do with the new high technology economy. But computers and computer components still have to be shipped to businesses and consumers, as do any goods purchased over the Internet.

The Dow Theory does not utilize the Dow Jones Utility Average (DJUA) which was introduced only in 1929, well after Charles Dow's death in 1902. However, we will argue below that the DJUA typically confirms moves in bond prices which in turn have major implications for stocks. A criticism of the Dow Theory—and most confirmation analyses—is that they are often late, coming after 20-30% of a move has already been made.

In Fig. 11-1 is shown a monthly chart of the DJIA with the DJTA directly below it. After the bear market in 1990, at no time during the 1990s did both averages dip below their most recent secondary trough. In 1992 while the DJTA dipped, the DJIA was moving sideways to up. Again in 1994, while the DJTA made a substantial retracement (though not below its 1992 low), the DJIA was again moving sideways. From the beginning of 1995, in what I refer to as the "new era" up trend, both averages steadily moved upward. The major difference in the averages was that because of the 1994 DJTA down move, this average took longer than the DJIA to reach new highs. Also at the end of 1997, while the DJIA was zigzagging down toward its new era up trendline, the DJTA made new all-time highs on its own. After that both averages surged to new all-time highs together.

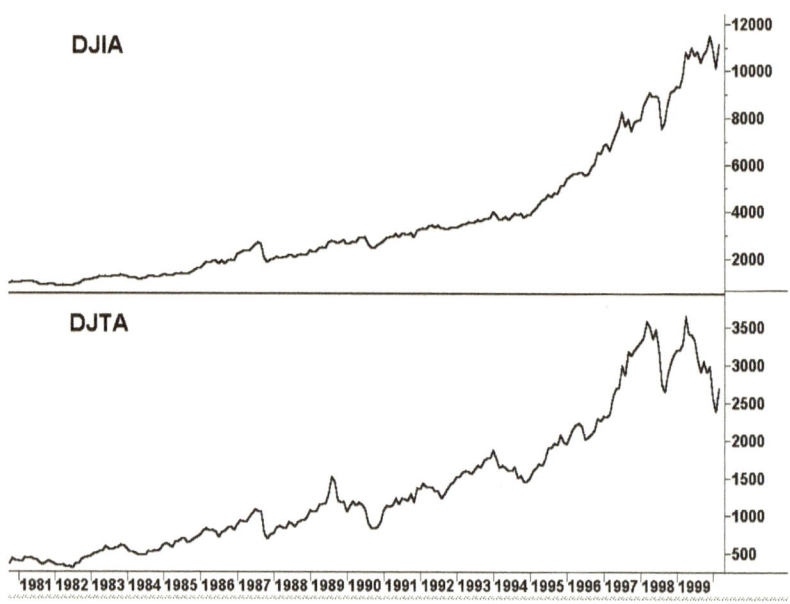

Fig. 11-1

No one knows for certain whether the extended bull market of the 1990s will continue or whether a major correction is in the cards. However, as a guide, if the transportation sector looks robust, then the DJIA is probably poised to move higher. If the transportation sector falters, then the wise course is to be cautious. In general, the larger the "divergence" between the DJIA and the DJTA, the more likely a correction in the index that is leading.

The Utilities Average

The Dow Jones Utilities Average (DJUA) is an index of 15 of the largest electric and gas utility companies in the United States. Many of the names you would recognize immediately. They are listed daily, along with a chart, in the MONEY AND INVESTING section of *The Wall Street Journal* under THE DOW JONES AVERAGES.

The first thing you should know about this index is that is has long been considered a proxy for the interest-rate environment. As bond prices move up (interest rates down), the DJUA typically moves up, too. This was true because utilities were known as stodgy companies with a chance for modest stock price appreciation but with hefty dividend yields. Thus, as interest rates decreased, owning utilities for fixed income purposes became more attractive.

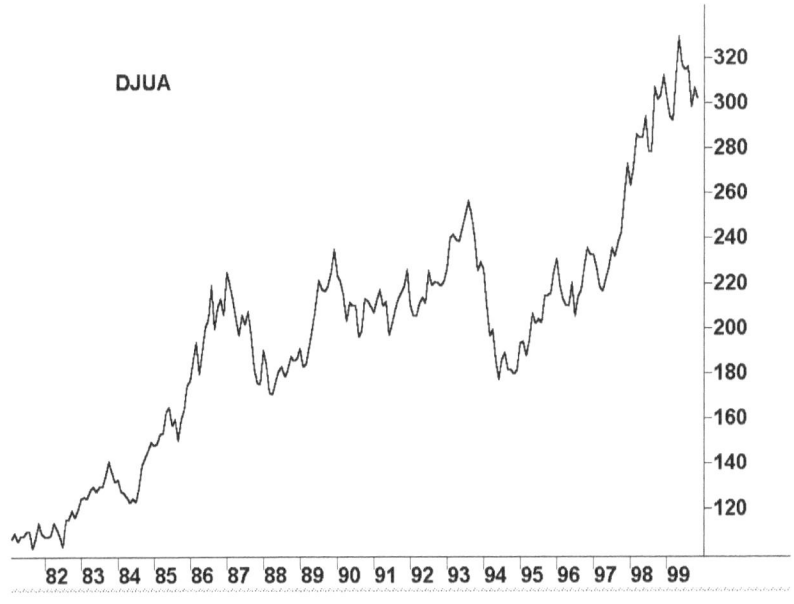

Fig. 11-2

Much of this perception of utilities has changed in recent years due to deregulation in the industry but also due to other factors, including those arising from nuclear power plant ownership and from managements having difficulty getting their acts together. This helps in part to explain the price action in Fig. 11-2. The DJUA made new highs along with the Dow Industrials into 1993, with the DJUA peaking at 256.66. This coincided with short-term interest rates at 3% and long bond yields under 6%. As interest rates rose into 1994, the DJUA fell to a low of 172.55, a nearly 33% decline. During this time, the Dow Industrials moved sideways to up. However, as bonds recovered into 1995 (in the case of the long bond from yields of over 8% to around 6%) the DJUA lagged far behind, a *non*-confirmation of the bond move. Then as the bond sputtered between 6 and 7% during much of 1996, the DJUA sputtered along with it. Then, in late 1997, as the long bond yield again approached 6%, the DJUA made all time highs, giving full confirmation to the bond rally. In technical analysis, "confirmations" between markets can be signals for powerful moves. As time proved, bonds rallied mightily with the long bond eventually hitting a low in yield of 4.69% during the global financial problems and the Long Term Capital Management hedge fund bailout culminating in October 1998.

Historically, bonds tend to lead the DJUA. In other words, if bonds rally (or decline), some time later the DJUA tends to rally (or decline). Usually, the shorter the time frame for this confirmation to occur, the more powerful the rally (or the decline). In contrast to bonds leading the DJUA, **the DJUA tends, historically, to lead the Dow Jones Industrial Average** (DJIA) and, hence, the broader stock market.

The Dollar Index

The late 1990s dollar strength was a reflection of the US's safe haven status in a world sometimes filled with financial turmoil, the attractive (and stable) US interest rate environment, and the great and enduring strength of the US economy. It is important to monitor the strength of the US dollar in terms of global currencies, because the strength of the dollar can influence so many other markets, including the US equity markets (direct correlation), the US bond markets (also a direct correlation) and the precious metals markets (an inverse correlation).

A convenient way to monitor the dollar is to watch the US Dollar Index. This index comprises a basket of 10 foreign currencies with strong representation by the Japanese yen, the euro and the British pound. A monthly chart of the US Dollar Index is shown in Fig. 11-3. From this plot you can see that the US dollar rally starting in early 1995 was impressive. And while the Index itself rose over 25% during that period, the US dollar versus some major currencies rose a great deal more than that. The Japanese yen moved from around 78 to near 130 to the dollar, a decline of 40% in dollar terms

Fig. 11-3

On the chart in Fig. 11-3 I've drawn in an up trendline for the 1995-1999 period. To put this rally into perspective, we should look further back along the time axis. With oil crises and inflation rampant in the 1970s, and the US bond market on the verge of collapse, the dollar had fallen on rather hard times. Enter Federal Reserve Chairman Paul Volcker. With a mandate to tame inflation, he forced short-term interest rates over the 17% level. Investors, realizing the Fed Chairman's resolve (and with those kinds of dollar denominated yields), sent the dollar soaring (the Volcker effect). The dollar stood so high, in fact, that the Reagan administration, fearing the impact on exports, made a push to weaken the dollar. At a meeting of the G7 countries it was boldly announced that a concerted effort to weaken the dollar would be undertaken. This is what I refer to as the G7 effect in Fig. 11-3.

Could the dollar again reach such lofty heights? Not likely in the absence of much higher interest rates. However, **should the dollar break above its multi-year highs, a 10% to 20% rise above the Index level of 100 is not outside the realm of possibility.** This would be very bullish for both stocks and bonds.

Keep an eye on the US Dollar Index. It is one of the keys to understanding the financial markets. While some may argue that the dollar is vastly overvalued, remember everything is relative in today's hot-money markets.

The CRB Index

An index helpful in intermarket analysis is the Bridge Commodity Research Bureau Futures Price Index, or more commonly, the CRB Index. It comprises a basket of 21 commodities, ranging from grains and meats and softs (cocoa, coffee and sugar) to energy and metals and industrials (copper, cotton and lumber). A frequently cited criticism of this index is its heavier weighting of the agricultural markets (62%) to non-food markets (38%), but it remains a good indicator for the direction of commodity prices.

In Fig. 11-4 is shown a monthly chart of the CRB index. Values are reported on a base year of 1967 = 100. The index reached a high near

340 in 1980, after the second energy embargo and coincident with the run-up in gold prices to over $850/oz. Many other commodities rose dramatically during that period, but not necessarily to their all-time highs. The Index fell all the way below 200 in 1986, with only an intermediate rally in 1984 that failed far below the all-time high. The rally from 1987 to 1989 broke the steep down trendline from 1980 but failed to exceed even the intermediate high of 1984. The subsequent decline—with another intermediate term rally—again reached the 200 level into 1993. The rally from 1993-94 looked promising, but peaked in 1996, slightly below the last major top in 1989. A secondary rally into the beginning of 1997 failed and finally violated the up trendline for this most recent advance. If you had stared at this chart long enough, you might have been tempted to conclude that the CRB Index was headed back to 200. In fact, the index fell to nearly the 180 level, with the Asian economic crisis contributing heavily to this decline.

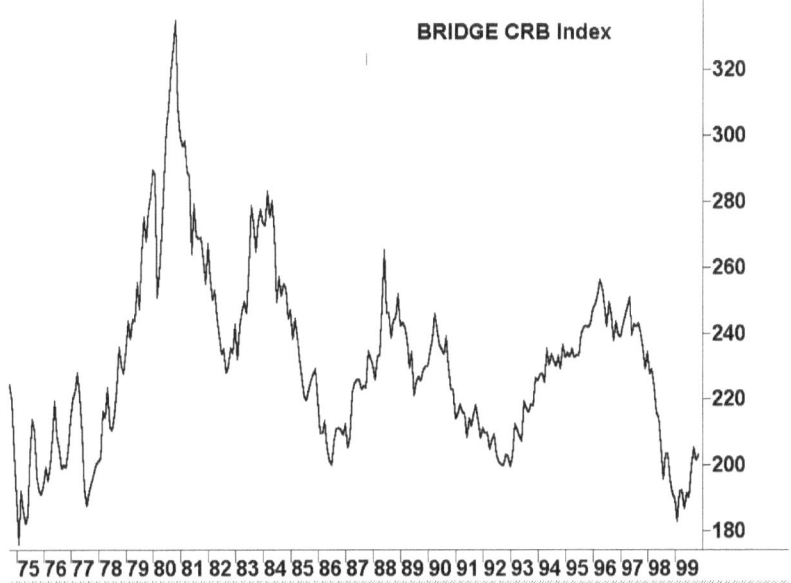

Fig. 11-4

Why bother with all this if we are not trading copper or cotton or grains? Because the direction of the CRB Index can give us insight into other markets. For example, if the CRB Index is in a down trend, there is little chance that gold will rally. At best gold may stay in a trading range, and we can feel confident that we do not have to rush in the market to buying gold mining stocks. On the other hand, if the CRB is in a definite up trend, gold is likely to get a boost and we may want to get more serious about accumulating those mining shares.

Also, commodity prices generally go in the opposite direction of bonds with commodities leading bonds. If the CRB index is declining, we should expect continued gains in bonds (lower yields). In turn, lower commodity prices and lower interest rates should be good for most companies' bottom lines, thus bullish for stocks. If the CRB index is rising, we should expect bonds to move lower in price (higher yields). Higher commodity prices and higher interest rates are not favorable to most companies' bottom lines (some exceptions might be mining or other natural resource companies), thus these trends are bearish for stocks.

Not all commodities making up the Index correlate closely with the Index at all times. In the late 1990s silver and palladium, which were driven by their own supply/demand pressures were going in the opposite direction of the Index.

The XAU

Another average that receives a good deal of attention is the Philadelphia Stock Exchange Gold/Silver Sector Index. This index is also known as the gold and silver index, the gold index, the XAU index, or most commonly as "the X-A-U." (The chemical symbol for the element gold is Au.)

The Philadelphia Stock Exchange (PHLX) was founded in 1790 as the first organized stock exchange in the US. It currently trades stocks, equity options, index options and currency options. Among its listed equity options are the LEAPS (*Long-term Equity AnticiPation Securities*) with expiration dates up to three years in the future. Among its index options are those on the semiconductor, airline, bank and oil service sectors.

The XAU, one of the best-known indices on the PHLX, is a capitalization-weighted index of 9 to 10 widely held gold and silver mining stocks. In early 2000 Canadian-based Barrick Gold (ABX—NYSE) had the heaviest weighting at about 29%. AngloGold Ltd. (AU—NYSE), a South African company, held the second largest weighting at just over 21%, followed by two other North American companies, Newmont Mining Corp. (NEM—NYSE) at 17% and Placer Dome Inc. (PDG—NYSE) at 12%. Together these four companies make up 79% of the index. The composition of this index had been in flux in the years leading up to 2000 due to acquisitions and the effect the dire state of the gold market had on some companies.

The XAU is important as an overall gauge of the gold mining stocks, but is also useful as a leading indicator of the gold price, and hence of inflation. In general, the mining stocks begin to rally before the price of gold. This makes sense when you consider that at the bottom of a decline in gold, much of the gold mining stock will be in "strong hands" (insiders and savvy professional investors). The insiders in the normal conduct of their business will be the first to observe supply/demand pressures. They will then push up stock prices by buying up what remaining shares are available, probably from long-suffering small investors who are only too happy to finally take a small profit or to recover some of their losses. On the contrary, at the top of the gold cycle, gold mining stocks will be in "weak hands" (speculators and diverse small investors, including mutual fund holders), and the XAU will not be a leading indicator for the subsequent drop in the price of gold. At best, near a top in the gold cycle, the XAU and gold mining shares will lose momentum and move sideways. However, as the gold price declines, the XAU and the mining stocks tend to decline rapidly.

In Fig. 11-5 is shown a monthly chart of the XAU since 1985. You can see from the many sharp peaks and valleys that this is, indeed, a very volatile sector. The sharp downward movement in the index beginning in 1996 corresponded to the steep downturn in the price of gold, with many central banks either selling or announcing plans to sell their gold during this period. Interestingly, while the gold price was hitting 20-year lows in 1999 the XAU actually moved off its 1998 lows. Whether this "divergence" has any significance, perhaps signaling a bottoming pattern in the XAU, remains to be seen.

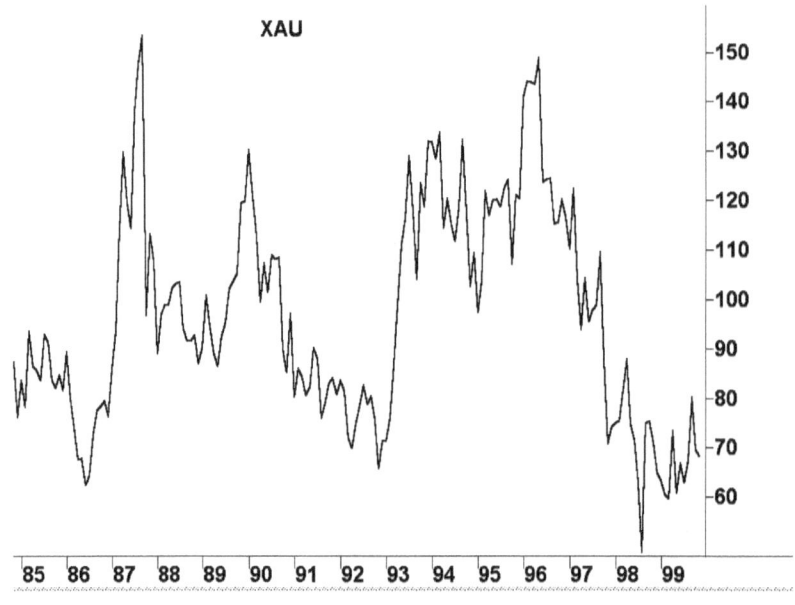

Fig. 11-5

Summary

In this chapter I have tried to introduce you to some of the most popular market averages outside of the large stock market indices. I have tried to emphasize throughout that these averages are important in that they give insight into what I refer to as "intra-market" dynamics. Strength (or weakness) in the transports usually implies strength (or weakness) in the industrials. Strength (or weakness) in utilities usually implies strength (or weakness) in bonds. Similar relationships exist for the other averaged discussed.

There are many other such averages, such as the banking index or the semiconducter index and, now, even various Internet indices. Depending on your particular tastes you may wish to follow these or other averages and try to understand their relevant intra-market dynamics.

Chapter 12

The Global Financial Architecture

In politics it is necessary to betray one's country or the electorate. I prefer to betray the electorate.

Charles de Gaulle

Most government leaders over the centuries, whether elected or not, have betrayed their constituencies by devaluing their countries' currencies.

The value of the US dollar in the global currency markets is the key to so many other markets including the US stock markets, the US bond market, and the precious metals. In a similar way any country's currency is often the key to its local financial markets. What the late 1990s proved was that the US dollar was the place to be. Experience from the 20th century, however, leads one to believe that this trend may not continue indefinitely into the next century. For much of the last half of the 20th century, the dollar generally fared poorly against other *major* currencies, such as the Swiss franc, the German mark and the Japanese yen. Why these currencies went through their late 1990s swoon was that the central banks of these respective governments, due to various economic considerations, had extremely lax monetary policies during this period. That kept the printing presses in those countries running overtime causing the supply of francs, marks and yen to increase and their value to decrease.

The 1997 currency crises in southeast Asia may have had slightly different origins—namely overextended loans denominated in US dollars and Japanese yen followed by a squeeze from foreign currency speculators—but the fundamentals were the same: too many baht, pesos, ringget and won being printed. The same was true in every country where the currency was under pressure, whether it was Russia (ruble), Brazil (real) or South Africa (rand). The printing presses were running overtime.

Why is the world in this currency predicament? Because the world's currencies (with the exception of the Swiss franc) are backed by…well, nothing. Some of the minor currencies pride themselves by being linked to the US dollar, but the dollar, in turn, is backed by, well…nothing. You can argue that the US is a great military power, owns Yellowstone National Park, and gives a home to both GE and Microsoft, among other national icons. But if you turn in your dollars to the government, you won't get a tank, a tree, a toaster or even software. The best you can expect is to get a bond, note or treasury bill—more paper for your paper. Before President Nixon was forced to take the United States off the gold standard in 1971 other governments, at least, could get gold for their dollars. Now they buy bonds, notes and t-bills instead.

Governments are renown for debasing their currencies. After banning individual ownership of gold in 1933, President Franklin Roosevelt, in a stroke of the pen, devalued the US currency from $20.67 per oz. of gold to $35 per oz. gold under the Gold Reserve Act of 1934. (Yes, those kinds of devaluations—approximately 40%—can happen in the USA.) In an attempt to introduce stability into the post-war era, the Allied powers in July, 1944 met in Bretton Woods, New Hampshire and agreed to make the dollar convertible to gold at this $35/oz. price and to make other currencies convertible to the dollar. This *Bretton Woods agreement*, though not without hiccups and not before seriously depleting the US government gold supply, remained in effect for 27 years. On Aug. 15, 1971 President Richard Nixon ended the exchange of dollars for gold, or in common parlance, "closed the gold window." His reasons for doing so were none too subtle. Foreign financial institutions had amassed dollar holdings of $36 billion (eurodollars) and US gold holdings amounted to only $18 billion. How could this imbalance have happened? In a sentence: the United States paid for the post World War II economic recovery while restraining communism and enjoying prosperity at home. We printed too many dollars.

What followed in 1973 was the "floating exchange" rate system, where currencies could fluctuate daily in the marketplace, their values deter- mined by millions of market participants. This system is the one still in place. To suggest that it has worked splendidly would be ludicrous. The constant fluctuations and uncertainties inherent in a floating exchange system are anathema to international commerce. This is a primary reason the European Union wants the euro to succeed. Since 1973 we've seen severe US and global inflation, the South American debt crisis, and many isolated examples of currency turmoil (Brazil and Russia moving their decimal points, for example, or the Mexican peso collapsing in 1994). What the floating exchange system led to was the 1997 currency fiasco in southeast Asia with economic instability spreading from there to other regions of the world. As I write in early 2000, China is rumored to be very close to devaluing its currency, and the Russia ruble is deemed virtually worthless. The discipline that is supposed to be dictated by the marketplace does not work when it comes to governments, because they can cheat for a long time before it catches up with them.

What I see happening in the not too distant future is a meeting of financial ministers in some bland locale, such as Turku, Finland. Out of this conference will come the "Turku Monetary Exchange Accords" in which the US dollar will be revalued with respect to gold and perhaps a number of other commodites, and all lesser currencies will be fixed to a basket of currencies composed of the US dollar, the euro, the Japanese yen and the Chinese yuan (renminbi). Or some similar agreement—you get the idea. Then any number of books by prominent economists and academicians will appear dissecting the history of the floating exchange era and lamenting the fact that the world suffered for so long under this archaic system. What does seem clear is that the world is long overdue for restructuring of its *currency foundation.*

The current buzz-phrase, of course, is "financial architecture." Global financial architecture refers to the entire gamut of financial structures—anything from banking to markets to hedging and derivatives, and globally from the International Monetary Fund to the World Bank to the Bank for International Settlements. But underlying this entire architecture is the global currency foundation. It is the currencies that have been the source of so much international economic turmoil. Without a stable currency foundation, the entire financial architecture is subject to tremors and in the extreme could come crashing down. Before I describe this global financial architecture, I present a speculation on how the global currency foundation might be restructured.

Perhaps the simplest scheme for the global currency foundation is to form three major currency zones. This is not an original idea. It has been bandied about in such prominent publications as the *Wall Street Journal, The Economist* and elsewhere. Just as the euro is now being used in the 11 countries of the European Monetary Union (EMU), so would all the countries of a given zone use the same currency. In fact, it is thought that the euro would be one of the currencies in use and that its reach would extend to Eastern Europe, perhaps the Middle East, and maybe even to Northern Africa, if not all of Africa (many of the African states are former European colonies). The conspiratoralists even claim that the euro is nothing more than a trial balloon to institute this "trilateral" currency regime. Naturally, the Western Hemisphere would use the US dollar (even now, Argentina is talking of "dollarizing" its currency). The Pacific region would use the "asian," which in the 1980s might have looked suspiciously like the yen, but nowadays might be an amalgamation of the yen, the Chinese yuan or renminbi, and any number of other Pacific currencies.

These three regional currencies might be linked in tight bands, or they could be allowed to float against one another. Any country not in one of the three zones would be at a distinct disadvantage in international transactions. I have not heard any explanations of what would become of the Swiss franc in such a currency-zone world, but presumably it would be absorbed into the euro—assuming the Swiss approved such a move in one of their famous referendums.

An advantage of this system would be the elimination of any "Thai bahts" that might be devalued, thus preventing a contagion of devaluations in a given region or currency zone. Also tighter monetary control from a *regional central bank* would help remove the temptation towards national cronyism that has led to mal-investment in areas of over capacity and also to outright corruption. The major disadvantage, especially from the viewpoint of major players like the United States, Japan and China, would be an individual country's loss of independence over their own monetary policy and to some degree over their own fiscal policy as well. After all, some limits on budget deficits and total debt would have to be enforced in order to maintain membership in the currency zone.

Would such a system work? It is difficult to predict. Certainly the costs of currency exchange within a given zone would drop to zero and the cost between zones would be reduced dramatically. At least initially this should be a deflationary factor and should benefit the consumer. The real test would come during a downturn in the economy, especially if such a downturn affected one region of a currency zone more dramatically than others.

What is surprising after the last two years of global currency turmoil is the lack of consensus about what to do about it. Walter Russell Mead, a senior fellow for US foreign policy at the Council on Foreign Relations, reported in the April 1999 issue of *Worth* on the then recent gathering of the world's elite in Davos, Switzerland. Here's a passage from that article: "What I wanted was to learn what the global establishment thinks about the future of the world's economic and political systems after the international financial crisis of the past year and a half. Had it all been just a blip on the screen? Might we still encounter serious trouble? Could we strengthen the system for the future? Short answers: The world's political and business leaders are seriously worried about the stability of the international economic system. They are deeply divided on what to do about it, too."

You will hear a lot more about fixing the global currency foundation in the next several years. Though the world's elite may be deeply divided on a solution, you can be sure they are all jockeying for their voices to be heard.

With this introduction as background, the remainder of this chapter gives a view of the global financial architecture near the beginning of the year 2000

The Bank for International Settlements

The Bank for International Settlements (BIS) was created in January 1930 at the Hague Conference, a main purpose of which was the settlement of German reparations after World War I. The BIS commenced activities in Basle, Switzerland on May 17, 1930. It is the world's oldest international financial organization. Known as the *banker to central banks*, it is indeed a bank, but one whose depositors are limited to central banks and international financial institutions. A significant portion of the world's foreign exchange reserves is held on deposit with the BIS.

The BIS has a legal structure of a limited company with an issued share capital. About 86% of the issued share capital is registered in the names of central banks, the remaining 14% being held by private shareholders. Shares trade on the Swiss exchange with individual shares priced in thousands of Swiss francs. All shares carry equal rights with respect to the annual dividend, but private shareholders may neither attend nor vote at the General Meetings since voting rights and representation are reserved for those central banks owning shares. In 1998, forty-five central banks had voting rights and representation at the General Meetings. However, some 120 central banks and international financial organizations use BIS as a bank. In addition, central bank officials from emerging-market economies are increasingly being invited to participate in discussions held at the BIS.

The Hague Agreements established the BIS as an international organization governed by international law with privileges and immunities necessary for the performance of its functions. The BIS has a legal status in Switzerland similar to other international organizations established there. It is subject neither to Swiss Federal Law concerning Banks and Savings Banks nor to the provisions of Swiss Company Law. The administration of the BIS is handled through the General Meeting, held annually on the second Monday in June, the Board of Directors and the Management. Since 1994, the Board has been composed of the six central bank Governors from the founding countries—Belgium, France, Germany, Italy, the United Kingdom and the US (the Federal Reserve is a central bank all but in name)—another member from each of these countries and the central bank Governors of Canada, Japan, the Netherlands, Sweden and Switzerland. These 11 countries are known as the *Group of Ten, or G-10* (yes, there are 11 of them). The Board appoints the General Manager and staff, numbering 463 from 29 countries.

One of the stated aims of the BIS is to promote cooperation of central banks and to provide additional facilities for international financial operations. It this way the BIS seeks to foster international financial stability. The bank also acts as Agent or Trustee in connection with various international financial agreements. In fact, one of its first functions was acting as Trustee in executing the Young Plan that arranged settlement of German reparations after World War I. The bank has acted as Trustee in a number of international loan agreements and as Collateral Agent to hold and invest collateral in the case of rescheduling of certain countries external debt. The BIS also acts as a center for monetary and economic research, primarily on questions of direct interest to central banks.

The BIS provides a forum for meetings of central bank officials on issues relevant to international monetary cooperation. The *Standing Committee of the Group of Ten central banks* has dealt with a series of issues on the Euro-currency markets. The *Basle Committee on Banking Supervision* considers specific supervisory problems and produced the 1988 agreement to achieve international convergence in the measurement of the adequacy of banks' capital and to establish minimum capital standards—ideas that are still evolving in Japan, China and many emerging countries. The *Committee on Payment and Settlement Systems* reviews developments in payment and settlement systems, including those for securities and foreign exchange market transactions. The BIS also hosts other international groups dealing with financial matters, such as the *Secretariat of the International Association of Insurance Supervisors.*

This should give you a staring point for what the BIS does. It is an important component in the international financial architecture.

The World Bank

Another wing of the global financial architecture is the World Bank (thereafter the Bank). It held its inaugural meeting in 1946 at Savannah, GA, where bylaws were adopted and executive directors were elected. Washington, D.C. was chosen as the site of the new institution. The Bank began formal operations on June 25, 1946. The Bank's first loan agreement was with France for $250 million for reconstruction purposes. In real terms it remains the largest loan ever made by the Bank. In 1946 the Bank had 38 member nations; today the Bank is owned by more than 180 member countries.

The operation of the Bank is carried out through a Board of Governors, with a governor from each member nation, and a Board of Executive Directors. The governors are usually ministers of finance or planning, and they meet at the Bank's annual fall meeting. They decide on key policy issues, changes in capital stock, and the admission or suspension of country members; they also endorse financial statements and budgets. But since they meet only once a year, the governors delegate powers to the Board of Executive Directors, 24 in all. These directors meet twice a week to oversee the Bank's business, which includes approving loans, the administrative budget, new policies, country assistance strategies, and borrowing and financial decisions. The president of the Bank chairs meetings of the executive directors and is responsible for the overall management of the Bank. The president, by tradition, has been from the United States, the Bank's largest shareholder, and is elected for a five-year renewable term.

The makeup of the Board of Executive Directors is as follows. The five largest shareholders—France, Germany, Japan, the United Kingdom and the US—each appoint an executive director. The remaining countries are represented by 19 executive directors who are elected by constituencies. Some countries have formed single country constituencies—for example, China, Russia and Saudi Arabia—while others have formed multi-country constituencies.

The principle stated mission of the Bank is to fight poverty "with passion and professionalism for lasting results." The Bank offers loans, advice and an array of customized resources to more than 100 developing countries and "countries in transition." The Bank is the world's largest provider of development assistance with approximately $20 billion in new loans each year. It also likes to think of itself as providing the knowledge to help each individual developing country onto a path of stable, sustainable growth. Those regions receiving substantial aid in recent years include East Asia and the Pacific, Latin America and the Caribbean, and Eastern Europe and Central Asia. Key sectors where recent lending is being targeted include water supply and sanitation, the environment, agriculture, urban development and transportation, education, health and nutrition, electric power and energy, the social and financial sectors, and public sector management.

You have most likely heard of some of the arms of the World Bank. The *International Bank for Reconstruction & Development* (IBRD) provides loans and development assistance to middle income countries and credit-worthy poorer countries. The IBRD accounts for three-fourths of the Bank's annual lending, which funds it raises in the debt markets through the sale of triple-A rated bonds. The IBRD loans are made at 75 basis points over what the Bank pays for funds. The loans must be repaid in 15-20 years. *The International Development Association* (IDA) provides interest free loans to the poorest countries. About 40 countries contribute to IDA's funding. Borrowers pay a fee of less than 1% to cover administrative costs, and loans must be repaid in 35-40 years with a 10-year grace period. Other arms include the *International Finance Corporation* which provides support to the private sector, the *Multilateral Investment Guarantee Agency* which encourages foreign investment, and the *International Centre for Settlement of Investment Disputes* which provides arbitration for investment disputes.

It is difficult to estimate how vital the World Bank really is. The Bank has a reputation of being highly political, but for the poorest countries the loans provided by the Bank are probably very important.

The International Monetary Fund (IMF)

The World Bank and the IMF were both established at the United Nations Monetary and Financial Conference held at Bretton Woods, New Hampshire in 1944. The **International Monetary Fund (IMF)** officially came into existence in December, 1945 when 29 countries signed its Articles of Agreement. The organization began formal operations in

March, 1947. For many years the World Bank and IMF occupied the same building in Washington, D.C. Today they are located on opposite sides of the street near the White House. They share a common library and other facilities, exchange economic data, and participate in other joint activities.

The operation of the IMF is very similar to that of the World Bank. The Board of Governors, composed of finance ministers or heads of central banks, one from each of the current 182 member nations, gather at an annual meeting. However, the day-to-day work of the IMF is delegated to a 24-member Executive Board. Eight Executive Directors represent a single country. These countries are: China, France, Germany, Japan, Russia, Saudi Arabia, the United Kingdom, and the United States. The other 16 Executive Directors represent groupings of the remaining countries. The Managing Director, who acts as chairman of the Executive Board, oversees a staff of around 2,600—only about a third the size of the World Bank. In contrast to the World Bank, where the Executive Director is from the United States, the Executive Director of the IMF is by tradition a European or other non-American.

While the World Bank borrows money in the debt markets, the IMF's resources come from quota subscriptions, or membership fees paid by the IMF's 182 member nations. The fees are proportionate to a country's economic size and strength. The accounting unit for the IMF is known as a Special Drawing Right (SDR). As of March, 1999, 1 SDR equaled approximately US $1.36. Whereas the World Bank lends only to credit-worthy governments of developing countries, any member country, rich or poor, has the right to obtain assistance from the IMF during those times when it is experiencing a shortage of foreign exchange. As of December, 1998, the IMF had credit outstanding to 60 countries for an amount of SDR 61.2 billion (about $83 billion).

While the World Bank was set up to aid in the reconstruction after World War II and to foster economic development in poorer nations, the IMF was established to promote international monetary cooperation and exchange stability. The Great Depression of the 1930s created a lack of confidence in paper money with many countries forced to abandon the gold standard. This situation led to confusion over currency exchange rates which, in turn, exacerbated the contraction of trade between nations. From the desire to address these problems grew the idea of an international institution that would monitor exchange rates, supply short-term financing for balance of payments adjustments, provide a forum for international monetary concerns, and extend financial and economic expertise to member countries.

The role of the IMF has expanded over the years. In the 1970s the steep run-up in oil prices along with strong inflationary pressures worldwide created many balance-of-payments problems for the developing nations. In response the IMF created an Oil Facility in 1974 to aid members in balance of payments difficulties. In the early 1980s the Latin American debt crisis forced the IMF into the role of "lender-of-last-resort" as well as a mediator between debtor nations and both creditor nations and private banks. The IMF was also instrumental in the Mexican bailout of 1994 and the southeast Asian currency crisis of 1997. The IMF has been roundly criticized, however, because of the stiff terms imposed on its loans. This *conditionality* for a nation's *stabilization program* includes targets or ceilings for bank credit, the budget deficit, foreign borrowing, external arrears, and international reserves. It has been suggested that the requirements imposed by the IMF in order to receive a loan can actually forestall an economic recovery in the affected nation.

Other Wings of the Global Financial Architecture

In addition to the Bank for International Settlements (BIS), the World Bank and the International Monetary Fund (IMF), there are many other elements to the global financial architecture. I describe some of these below, noting that the list is by no means complete.

First I mention the *G7* group of industrialized countries. This "*Group of Seven*" includes Canada, France, Germany, Italy, Japan, the United Kingdom, and the United States. At the much-ballyhooed G7 summits these countries sometimes discuss economic issues or make decisions on currency interventions. In recent years Russia has been invited to join the G7 summits, prompting writers to use the term "G8" or the phrase "Summit of the Eight." Russia in 2000 hardly qualifies as an economic power, but it is still a military power because of its huge nuclear arsenal. The G7/G8 summits can address a wide range of topics including global and political issues. These meetings seem to provide G8 leaders with photo-ops for hand shaking and broad smiles, but often produce little other than pretentious "communiqués."

There is also the *G10*, or "*Group of Ten*," which is based in Basle, Switzerland at the BIS (see above). The G10 actually has eleven members which include the basic seven from the G7 plus Belgium, the Netherlands, Sweden and Switzerland. The G10 came about as a group of countries agreeing to make resources available to the IMF outside their quotas. The G10 has been a forum for discussion of international monetary questions and, in conjunction with the G10 central banks, for pursuing international financial stability.

There has also been an attempt by President Clinton to form a "*G22*" group, an informal set of representatives from 22 developed and developing countries. In 1998 this group prepared working papers on transparency, strengthening financial sectors and dealing with crises. These working papers have become the unofficial basis for the redesign of the global financial architecture.

There are a number of other groups that are important in the global financial picture. The *Basle Committee on Banking Supervision* (also residing at the BIS) has produced the Basle Concordat, or Basle Capital Accord, which is a set of minimum standards for the supervision of international banking groups and their cross-border establishments. These standards are intended to enhance standards of supervision especially in relation to solvency and thereby to strengthen the soundness and stability of international banking.

The *International Accounting Standards Committee* (IASC), located on Fleet Street in London, aims to achieve uniformity in the accounting principles that are used by businesses and other organizations for financial reporting around the world. Global accounting standards allow for more efficient resource allocation by investors, business leaders and government decision-makers.

The *International Organization of Securities Commissions* (IOSCO), with its General Secretariat located in Montreal, has established standards for international securities transactions. Their goal is to maintain just, efficient and sound markets, to set up effective surveillance and to act as an effective enforcement against offenses.

There are also some informal elements of the global financial architecture. The so-called *Paris Club* is a meeting between representatives of a developing country that hopes to restructure its official debt and representatives of any creditor nations and/or international banking institutions. Such meetings usually transpire after a developing country has difficulty meeting its interest payments. These meetings are traditionally chaired by a senior official of the French Treasury Department, hence the "Paris Club" designation.

These are some of the participants in the present structure of the global financial architecture. Some would argue that I should also include institutions such as the Federal Reserve and the European Union, or others like the World Trade Organization (WTO), NAFTA, the Organization for Economic Co-operation and Development (OECD) and a whole host of other alphabetically labeled organizations. No doubt these organizations are extremely important regarding monetary, economic and trade policy. My objective in this chapter, however, is to make you familiar with the major players in the global financial architecture circa 2000.

Problems that all these institutions face are the speed and size of modern monetary transactions. A trillion dollars in currency transactions alone occur daily, and a few clicks of a mouse can sent huge assets fleeing a small economy. These, along with financial transparency and trying to maintain national sovereignty in the face of financial regulation and access to global capital markets will continue to challenge the present system or any restructured global financial architecture.

References

1. *The Economist* (see Chapter 1), especially the January 30, 1999 issue.
2. *Business Week* (see Chapter 1), February 8, 1999.

Chapter 13

Conspiracies, Gurus and Such

Combinations of wickedness would overwhelm the world by the advantage licentious principles afford, did not those who have long practiced perfidy grow faithless to each other.

Samuel Johnson

Conspiracies

Conspiracies, or appearances of conspiratorial plotting, sometimes seem to be a crucial part of the investing scene. There are newsletters and books devoted to such interpretations. Even one of the books I recommend you read, namely Ted Warren's *How to Make the Stock Market Make Money for You*, could leave a person with the impression that Wall Street and the other financial markets are nothing more than a huge conspiratorial plot.

Personally, as a sometimes novelist, I enjoy conspiracies. In fact, I own a small library on the subject and have probably done more reading about such machinations than the average person. Does this make me an expert on the subject. No. But it does give me some fuel to express an opinion.

Do I believe in conspiracies? Sure. Conspiracies have been common throughout history and exist today. Should you as a whole investor be concerned about each and every conspiracy and adjust your portfolio accordingly? I don't think so.

The primary "global" conspiracies that would seem to affect the whole investor swirl around the creation of the Federal Reserve and the Fed itself, the Trilateral Commission, the Council on Foreign Affairs, and the Bilderbergers.

With regard to the Federal Reserve, it is theorized that a cabal of international bankers backed the presidency of Woodrow Wilson whom they were able to manipulate because of his personal indiscretions. With Wilson as their pawn they forced through the creation of the Federal Reserve with its fractional money system and its fiat money. While they were up to their mischief they were able to institute the national income tax as well—and I do admit to cursing Wilson for this act every year. What is often not mentioned in these stories is the system before the creation of the Federal Reserve. Each bank issued its own currency which was supposed to be backed by gold or silver. However, not all banks were as stable or well run as every other bank, and a run on a poorly managed bank would lead to runs on well-managed banks with a resultant calamitous upset in the economy. It was precisely to prevent such bank runs and such large swings in the economy that the "central bank" was established.

Did vested interests profit from the establishment of the Federal Reserve? Of course. Vested interests profited from decisions made in Babylonian times and during the rule of the Egyptian pharaohs and at the peak as well as decline of the Roman Empire. Vested interests will profit from decisions made in the new millennium. It's the way human history works and we have to live with it.

Today most of us, unless we have just finished reading about a conspiracy theory or have just read some newsletter writer who tells us about our worthless fiat currency, blandly go about using Federal

Reserve notes and are happy as a lark to receive them, even it they are only credited as arrangements of electrons on a magnetic disk in a bank computer. And even if there are traces of truth to the conspiracy theories—after all, with something as monumental as creating a central bank all kinds of Congressional and White House intrigues will be involved—and even if a newsletter writer is correct about our fiat currency, what effect really is this going to have on our investment outlook? True, you can buy a few bullion or numismatic coins and get some money into a hard currency like the Swiss franc, but this is just prudent diversification anyway, and has been advised elsewhere in this guide. But the Federal Reserve system is here to stay, and Federal Reserve notes are here to stay in one form or another (our hundreds, fifties and twenties have recently changed appearance) until the time that the United States government would cease to exist, in which case we would have much more serious problems on our hands anyway. In the meantime don't let these theories influence your choice of a good insurance program, good stock and bond selection along with some coins and a foreign currency or two, and, oh yes, while we're at it let's try to maximize our return on those good old fiat Federal Reserve notes.

With regard to the Trilateral Commission, it does exist. The North American office (includes the US and Canada) address is:

The Trilateral Commission
345 East 46th Street
New York, NY 10017
(212)-661-1180
www.trilateral.org

You can write to them or call them. You can receive information about the organization and publications from them. This doesn't seem so secret to me. There is a European office in Paris and a Japanese office in Tokyo. This is where the "trilateral" comes from. The Commission was set up to encourage mutual understanding and closer cooperation among these three regions of the world.

Who are the members of the Trilateral Commission? Well, it is true that David Rockefeller was instrumental in founding the commission. Herein lies the source of many conspiracy theories—the mere mention of the Rockefeller name conjures up images of such intrigues. The commission's association with sometimes shadowy figures such as Henry Kissinger and Zbigniew Brzezinski does not calm the conspiracy buffs either. But who belongs. Well, I don't. But then I don't run in the same circles as David Rockefeller. Mr. Rockefeller is probably not going to want to consult on major world problems with Ben who pumps gas at the corner service station or Megan who works at the local daycare, either. No, Mr. Rockefeller probably prefers leaders in government, business and finance, and leading intellectuals from academia. These are precisely the people who belong to the Trilateral Commission. That some writers find something sinister in this strains my own credulity.

Do members of the Trilateral Commission have no self-interests? Of course they do. Do members of the Commission ever exploit their membership in such a distinguished group? Of course they do. Henry Kissinger and Zbigniew Brzezinski are two good examples. Do no members ever try to influence the group to benefit their own countries or governments or companies?

Of course they do. These people may be wealthy and powerful, but they are human beings after all. They no doubt want to become wealthier and more powerful.

Suppose you belong to one of your town's major charitable organizations. You may not have joined for the express purpose of exploiting business connections, but if Frank wants to give you some business because he knows you are in the organization and likes you, you are not going to turn him down. I doubt anyone would say there is a conspiracy involving you and Frank and the charitable organization just because you take his business.

But some will argue that these people want to take over the world. Don't be ridiculous. The world is already their personal bowl of cherries. These people have available to them travel, communications and luxuries that kings and rulers of yesteryear could not even have imagined. They have access to government, business and academic leaders and many if not most have fabulous wealth. Imagine for an instance what a lifestyle change an extra $10,000 a month would do for you. Now imagine hundreds of millions or even a billion dollars of wealth. It's difficult to really comprehend. These people are not concerned about next month's mortgage or the kids' tuition bill. They lead a different life, with correspondingly different duties and responsibilities, than you or I do, and that's why you and I are not asked to join their club.

But can you imagine these people wanting to upset the status quo? If anything, I can imagine these people wanting to make things even better for their children and the generations that follow. I find it hard to believe that they want to spread revolution, war or pestilence because such things tend to upset the status quo. Besides you have in such an organization tremendous egos interacting. I should think that alone would temper schemes from ever going too far in one direction, and in particular in a direction favoring one or a few individuals.

Also a question arises as to why so many of our Secretaries of State and other cabinet members come from the ranks of the Council on Foreign Affairs. But who belongs to the Council on Foreign Affairs? Those individuals who are most expert on foreign matters. I mean, do you really want Jake Smith who operates a bicycle factory at the edge of town and who occasionally sends a shipment to Japan or Taiwan to be running our State Department? Better we have someone who has studied this subject in exhaustive detail and who knows and has interacted with other experts in this area.

The Bilderbergers, so-called because of the hotel in the Netherlands where they first met, is another group around which many conspiracy theories swirl. A couple of the supposed more sinister aspects of this group is the extreme secrecy of their annual meetings and the news suppression of these meetings by the media. Also this group is supposed to "interview" or "okay" new heads of state, such as Bill Clinton's invitation to the meeting the year before he won the Democratic nomination for president. The composition of this group is made up of European royalty, some with lineages into the middle and dark ages, extremely wealthy individuals, media moguls, and government leaders. Naturally there is some crossover from the Trilateral Commission.

The Bilderbergers are supposed to be the real group behind the push for one world government, with the Trilats, the UN, the CIA, the Mossad and all sorts of foundations and think tanks doing their dirty work for them. I do not have an address for the Bilderbergers nor will I profess to be an expert on them. Yet, considering the makeup of the group, it is difficult for me to believe that if someone were planning a takeover of the world or planning to control the world that others in the group would not object. It is also difficult for me to believe that with such egos involved that they could all be induced to think in like terms on such a weighty matter as global domination without regard to individual self-interests showing through. Do they have influence? Yes. Do they have a say in national and international affairs? Yes. Do they control the popular media? Yes, to a large degree. Do they have agendas? Yes. But do they control world events? Not likely. If they did, why don't they stop the proliferation of the internet and electronic bulletin boards, and newsletters and magazines and books and television. These are the things that are anathema to conspiracies and secrecy and plots to take over the world. Why don't they crush entrepreneurship? Certainly 15 to 20 years ago, Bill Gates, the founder and CEO of Microsoft, was not a member of these groups. As I write this he is reputedly the wealthiest man on earth. I don't know whether he now belongs to any of these groups, but he would probably be welcome.

Have I proven anything? No. But I want to put your mind at ease. I want you to sleep at night without worrying about such groups at the Trilateral Commission and the Bilderbergers. From some of the mailings I receive—I think I am permanently on every investing-related mailing list in the country—it seems that some writers would have you withdraw from every investment you own, put all your money into gold or silver and convince you to store it in a hole in your backyard. All this in anticipation of a global takeover by elitists, crazed environmentalists and devil worshippers. What I'm saying is don't let these kinds of rantings and ravings prevent you from living a normal life with normal investing goals. Don't allow them to create inaction on your part by not taking part in an exciting investment world.

If one or more of the above mentioned organizations were indeed involved in a major conspiracy to take over the world, I contend, even with a controlled media, that troop movements and armament flows and infiltration networks would be detectable and would be broadcast all over the internet and probably even on CNN. But true believers will say that I don't understand: that these groups have been undermining our society for decades, that they already control Congress and the White House and the CIA, that they plan a takeover from within by undermining our educational system and poisoning our children's minds with environmental gobbledygook, gender and racial equality, sex education and so forth, and oh yeah, don't forget about the black helicopters..., etc., etc.

I can't answer every objection here. I don't agree with a lot that passes as generally accepted in the 1990s. But I can remember back to the 1960s, a time of student protest and general civil unrest. It seems to me that much of what now is generally accepted behavior—liberal sexual attitudes, liberal divorce, liberal educational standards, liberal dress and grooming standards, liberal standards of behavior, liberal freedom of expression and gutter language, drug use, and on and on—was opposed by none other than the conservative elitist establishment. That's right— can you imagine it?—all this opposed by the insiders.

Who wanted it? The people. In particular the babyboomers, who have imposed their will on us now for oh so long, wanted it. (Having been born one year before the official start of the babyboom era, I excuse myself from this group.) They wanted freedom from all the usual societal constraints. Indeed, they demanded it. By their sheer numbers they forced many dubious freedoms upon society. With freedom, however, also comes responsibility. This, unfortunately, they neglected to impose. Of course, by now, some of these babyboomers have become actual insiders. They have been able to place like-minded people on the courts, into positions of power in government and have them promoted to prominence in academia. We don't have to look to the Trilateral Commission or the Bilderbergers for conspiracies to explain the sad state of contemporary society. All we have to do is look inside ourselves and acknowledge what we have allowed to transpire.

Financial Newsletters

There are many interesting newsletters available, even some where you can learn something useful. The majority of newsletter writers, however, do not have a good track record with regard to investment advice. Often they, like the rest of the investing public, climb on board an investment trend well after a significant move has been made, or they try to be clever and in a contrarian move suggest something that has fallen completely out of favor. The problem with contrarian picks, however, is that an investment that has fallen out of favor may have done so for fundamental reasons, and these picks do not always return to favor in a timely manner.

Another group of newsletter writers recommends penny stocks— stocks that sell for less than a dollar or sometimes less than $2—with the allure that one of these diamonds in the rough is the next Intel or

Microsoft. Occasionally a penny stock does take off for a while and produces impressive results. The problem is that the newsletter writer apparently expects us to make a sizable commitment to each of his numerous picks, because you only hear about how much this one successful pick would have returned if only you had invested $10,000. These same writers seldom mention what would have happened to those other $10,000 commitments in the not-so-successful picks.

Investment newsletters fall into a broad range of categories. Most give investment advice on specific stocks and the stock market in general, but many are sector specific, while some are geared to particular markets such as currencies, the metals or commodities. A few might even come on as the communiqué of a secret society whose members' sole objective is the accumulation of wealth. Some are geared more toward political commentary and some towards conspiracy theories. Some are the so-called "gloom and doomers" that forecast this or that calamity waiting to befall the financial markets or mankind in general. Most will give such a broad range of investment picks that some are bound to be right. To their credit many newsletter publishers will send you a sample copy, and most will refund your entire subscription fee after a few trial months and allow a prorated refund after that time.

I'm not saying that you should never read any financial newsletters or that you cannot get investing ideas from them. Many of these newsletter writers are very clever and witty, and many can write very well. Just be wary of accepting everything they say on faith. My caution to you, as a whole investor, is: always do your own due diligence before committing any money.

Financial Gurus

When I refer to gurus, I'm not referring to all financial newsletter writers or financial media commentators. Gurus are those investment advisors who have attained an almost cult status and whose followers plunge into and out of markets on the whims of these financial deities. The really powerful gurus are those that can actually move markets.

In the very early 1980s Joe Granville had this effect on the stock market before he missed the big rise in equities during the first term of the Reagan administration. He subsequently became nothing more than a conversation piece. He is still attempting a comeback.

Robert Prechter who championed the Elliott Wave Principle, an esoteric technical theory, became a guru for the 1980s when he correctly predicted the huge rise in stock prices in that decade. Ralph Nelson Elliott, who formulated the Elliott Wave Principle in the 1930s and 1940s and who passed on shortly thereafter, became a "dead guru" due to Prechter's success. The Elliott Wave Principle, in a sentence, is a theory that all heavily traded markets in all time frames move in a series of five waves up, then a series of three waves down. There is no question that the theory has an intellectual appeal or that it appears to work in some situations. However the configuration of some waves leaves much to be desired, and the interpretations used to mold these structures into the desired forms can stretch the imagination. In any case Mr. Prechter was frightened off by the 1987 stock market crash and has been on the wrong side of the Great Bull Market run ever since. Needless to say, his status as a guru has been badly tarnished. I should mention that other authors have taken up the banner of the Elliott Wave Principle, notably Glenn Neely. It is noted that Mr. Prechter has merely been the victim of an incorrect wave count.

Another dead guru is W.D. Gann. His methods involve cycles, geometric angles, "master time factors" and some say mysticism. Gann's methods are applied to both the stock and futures markets and can be extremely tedious and obscure. He still has a large following. Legends surround anyone who is thought to have had great success in the financial markets. So it was with Mr. Gann. Reports are that he made over a $100 million during his lifetime, but this has not been proven. Others contend that he died with relatively little in assets and that his fame came primarily from self-promotion and that what wealth he had came primarily from his clients.

Elaine Garzarelli attained guru status after she correctly called the 1987 stock market crash. (Many others claim to have called it, but she actually did.) Her methods involve a large number of economic indicators which in combination help predict the direction of the stock market. She continued to have great success until the summer of 1996 when she told her followers to exit the stock market. She and they subsequently missed the next 1,500 points of the present bull run. Though she seems to be prospering, it may require another stunning call for her to regain her guru status.

Others who would be considered gurus if, in fact, they were newsletter writers or investment advisors include Warren Buffett and George Soros. Warren Buffett is the chairman of Berkshire Hathaway, a holding company which in reality is a huge closed-end mutual fund, and George Soros is the head of the Quantum Fund, an international hedge fund. These renowned investors have made fortunes that would dwarf even the $100 million supposedly made by Gann. Both Buffett and Soros have moved markets when any word leaks that either has established an investment position. However, in any interviews, both men are extremely careful not to allow any hint of their investment plans.

To end this section, I again must mention Alan Greenspan and the Federal Reserve. No, Mr. Greenspan or the other members of the Fed are not, strictly speaking, gurus. However, in the 1990s, Mr. Greenspan and the Federal Reserve have attained a cult status. This is somewhat of a carryover from Paul Volcker's reign as chairman of the Fed. Mr. Volcker, an imposing figure at six feet seven inches tall, is credited with taming the high inflation of the late 1970s and early 1980s. Mr. Greenspan, a long-time inflation hawk, is credited with keeping inflation low while at the same time keeping the economy growing slowly. This combination is nirvana for the stock market. Consequently, Mr. Greenspan is given credit for the Great Bull Market run in stocks, but clearly corporate profits, the technology/information revolution, and the emergence of a global economy have had a hand in it as well.

The story of inflation is not so straightforward either. No one questions that Mr. Volcker and Mr. Greenspan have done a masterful job of running the Federal Reserve, but they were aided in the inflation fight during the 1980s and 1990s by a deflation in commodity prices that were terribly overextended in price at the end of the 1970s. Furthermore, the opening up of emerging markets in Latin America, Southeast Asia and Eastern Europe has, at least as of this writing, kept a cap on wage prices. Finally, the financial markets have been willing so far to absorb the debt securities of the US government and those of most other sovereign nations. Whether all these scenarios will continue remains to be seen.

The point of this entire section is threefold. First if you are involved in investing for any length of time, you are bound to run into the names of the people discussed above. I thought you should at least be aware of them. Second, I hope I've pointed out with sufficient exposition that gurus come into favor and fall out of favor. As long as they correctly predict the markets they are adored. As soon as they make a wrong call they become also-rans. In the 1970s, when interest rates were skyrocketing, even the Federal Reserve was not universally loved as it is today.

Finally, I want to recommend that you do **not** follow the teachings, practices or pontifications of a guru. Become your own person when investing. Study the markets, learn the language, know when prices are high or low, research companies, and so forth. Investing is not easy. There are no secret formulas or magic systems. If someone offers you one, be suspicious and refuse. The key to successful investing is developing a disciplined methodology as outlined in Chapter 1—learn your investing temperament, obtain knowledge before investing, diversify into different investment classes as well as within investment classes, and stick to a strict money management system.

References

1. Antony C. Sutton and Patrick M. Wood, *Trilaterals over Washington*, Vols. I & II, The August Corporation, Scottsdale, AZ, 1981. (These are out of print—check your local library.)

2. Gary Allen, *None Dare Call It Conspiracy*, Concord Press, Kailua-Kona, HI, 1972.

3. Larry Abraham, *Call It Conspiracy*, Double A Publications, Wauna, WA, 1985.

4. Texe Marrs, *Circle of Intrigue*, Living Truth Publishers, Austin, TX, 1995.

5. Michael Baigent, Richard Leigh and Henry Lincoln, *Holy Blood, Holy Grail*, Dell Publishing Co., New York, NY, 1983.

6. John J. Robinson, *Born in Blood—The Lost Secrets of Freemasonry*, M. Evans & Company, New York, NY, 1989.

7. Robert R. Prechter, Jr. And A. J. Frost, *Elliott Wave Principle*, New Classics Library, Gainsville, GA, 1990.

8. Glenn Neely, *Mastering Elliott Wave*, Windsor Books, Brightwaters, NY, 1990.

9. Kenneth L. Fisher, *100 Minds That Made the Market*, Business Classics, Woodside, CA, 1993.

10. Robert G. Hagstrom, Jr., *The Warren Buffett Way*, John Wiley & Sons, Inc., New York, NY, 1994.

11. George Soros, *The Alchemy of Finance*, John Wiley & Sons, Inc., 1994.

12. Mark Hulbert, Editor, *The Hulbert Financial Digest*, The Hulbert Financial Digest, Inc., Alexandria, VA (monthly newsletter that rates the performance of a large number of other newsletters—703-683-5905).

13. Norman G. Fosback, Editor, *Investor's Digest*, The Institute for Econometric Research, Deerfield Beach, FL (monthly newsletter featuring quotes and stock picks from selected newsletters—800-442-9000).

Appendix 1

Sector Investing

> In anguish we uplift
> A new unhallowed song:
> The race is to the swift;
> The battle to the strong.
>
> John Davidson, *War Song*

Introduction

Some pundits advocate "sector investing." A sector is a group of industries having similar fundamental characteristics. An **industry** is a collection of companies with similar primary lines of business. The Standard and Poors (S&P) 500 divides its 500 companies into 90 industries and 11 sectors. These sectors are:

> Basic Materials
> Capital Goods
> Consumer Cyclical
> Consumer Staples
> Energy
> Financials
> Services

Technology
Transportation
Utilities
and "Other"

The S&P 500 Consumer Cyclical sector, for example, includes 21 industries that range from Auto Parts to Homebuilding, Restaurants, and even Toys. The S&P 500 also divides companies into four broad-based **segments**: the Industrials, Financials, Transportation and Utilities issues. In contrast, *Investor's Business Daily (IBD)* identifies 197 "Industry Groups" (those stocks on the major exchanges—not limited to 500 companies). Many writers, myself included, loosely apply the term "sector" to refer to an S&P 500 industry or to one of *IBD*'s more narrowly defined Industry Groups.

Sector investing, also called sector rotation, means rolling money from one S&P 500 sector to another as the economy moves through the different phases of its cycle. For example, at the start of an economic expansion, "early cycle" stocks such as capital goods and transportation companies may fare better, while in a contraction phase "defensive" stocks such as consumer cyclical and financial companies may do better.

A Way to Invest in "Sectors"

With the proliferation of mutual funds in the 1980s and 90s, many funds now offer opportunities to invest in broad sectors and also in some rather narrow industry groups. In fact, rolling money from one industry group fund to another seems to be replacing the more traditional sector investing. You shoud note, however, that some industry groups have cycles that are only loosely connected to, or are independent of, the larger macro economy.

It sometimes seems there must be Wall Street cliques who determine when a particular sector or industry group is hot (or cold). What is clear is that when some area is designated "hot," then glee and adoration flow to those stocks. Only woe and consternation flow to a sector that is "cold." Even mundane groups, such as paper or insurance stocks can get hot, but more often than not hot groups occur in technology or technology-related areas. Sectors that are very hot are often the same ones that eventually become very cold and *vice versa*. A couple of extreme examples in recent years include: (1) the Internet stocks, which in early 1997 were sitting there, doing relatively little, while in 1998 money could not be thrown at them fast enough; and (2) the oil service group which in 1997 was red hot, but which for most of 1998 was frozen solid, dead cold.

Another example of a hot industry group from late summer 1998 to early 2000 was biotechnology (this group was also very hot circa 1993). You have probably heard of the success stories like Genentech, Chiron or Amgen, but do we invest in these more established companies or do we try a few of the medium- and small-sized bio-tech firms that may soar in value but whose risk is great? Picking the right ones seems a daunting task. This is where a fund like **Fidelity's Select Biotechnology Portfolio** (see Figure A1-1) comes in. They will do the picking, you merely watch the industry group.

According to the 1999 *Fidelity Select Portfolios Annual Report*, there are 40 such "sector funds" to pick from, all at the same mutual fund company, anything from Air Transportation to Utilities Growth (sorry, nothing starting with a "Z"). There is a 3% load for new money into the Fidelity Select Portfolios funds. However, once money is in the Select Portfolio universe it is "tracked" by Fidelity so that there are no additional load fees applied if you switch to another Select fund. This is true of reinvestment funds as well as your original outlay. You may also switch into and out of a money market fund without incurring new load fees. Initial minimum investment is $2500 ($500 for a retirement account).

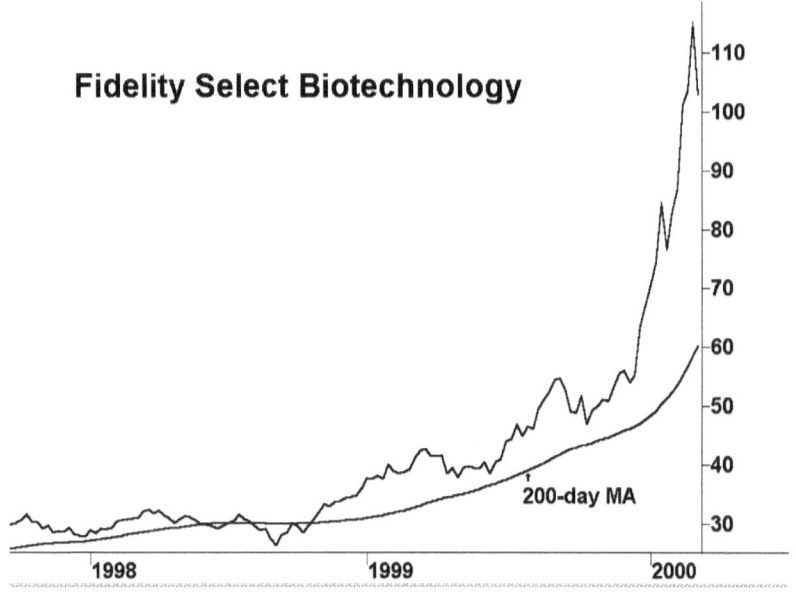

Fig. A1-1

A strategy for using the Fidelity funds might be to study a half-dozen or so Select funds of interest to you. Diversify as much as possible across sectors as defined above. You might follow these funds by charting their daily or weekly prices (net asset values or NAVs). You could use trendlines or support/resistance levels, for example, to determine when to switch from one fund to another. If you own a computer, you could actually follow all 40 funds quite easily and even apply, say, 200-day (40-week) moving averages or other indicators that might be appropriate for the more volatile funds. For less volatile funds a reasonable strategy might be to move into (out of) a fund when it crosses above (below) its 200-day moving average. To follow these funds on a computer, you may need charting software and maybe even a data provider.

If you want to play the "sector investing" game, the Fidelity Select Portfolios is as good a place as any to park some of your speculative money. This investing approach is not necessarily for everyone. It certainly is not for those with a buy-and-hold temperament, even though you could be in some of these funds for years before getting a sell signal. Neither should it be assumed that there are no dangers to this investing approach. It is certainly possible you could get caught in the trap of switching into hot funds right when they are ready to turn over and move down.

If this approach interests you, Fidelity can be reached at:

Fidelity Investments
P. O. Box 1284
Boston, MA 02104
(800)-544-8888
www.fidelity.com

Many other fund families will give you the opportunity to switch into and out of "sector funds." I suggest that you stick to the most solid fund families such as those mentioned in Chapter 6.

References

1. Sam Stovall, *Sector Investing*, McGraw-Hill, New York, NY, 1996.

2. *Investor's Business Daily* (IBD), 12655 Beatrice Street, Los Angeles, CA 90066. (800)-831-2525. (IBD offers a two-week free trial subscription.)

Appendix 2

Support and Resistance

Past and to come seem best; present worst.

Shakespeare, *Henry IV*

There exist some simple technical concepts that can help the investor decipher whether the past, present or future is best or worst. In this appendix, we emphasize two of the most important and fundamental concepts in market technical analysis, namely **support** and **resistance**. Understanding these concepts will (1) allow you to enter trades at opportune times and (2) make you aware of when to exit positions either before giving back too much of your profit or before taking too large a loss on a losing position. This notion of not giving back too much profit or of limiting losses is rarely covered in discussions on investing or trading, but are crucial considerations that should be emphasized.

Support and Resistance

Support is a price level were buying interest overcomes selling pressure. Support is most frequently encountered at levels where troughs or low points occur on a price chart.

Resistance is a price level where selling pressure overcomes buying interest. Resistance is most frequently represented on charts at price peaks.

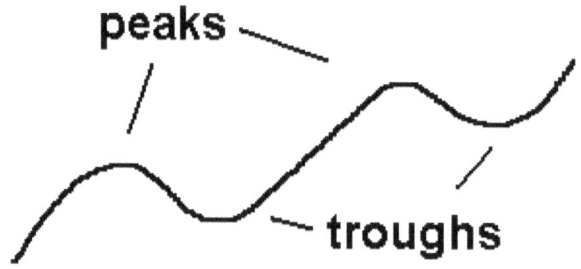

Fig. A2-1

The reason price support occurs when prices return to the level of a previous trough is because bullish investors see an opportunity to increase or initiate a position at what in retrospect represented a good price. Bearish investors who sold short at the previous trough and who suffered while the price level increased, now have a chance to get out of their positions at or near even money. Thus, at a support level, both bulls and bears will be buying.

The reason price resistance occurs when prices return to a previous peak is because bulls who bought at this peak and who suffered through a downturn now see their chance to recapture their money. Bears, on the other hand, see an opportunity to increase or initiate a position at what once represented a good selling opportunity. Thus, at resistance levels both bulls and bears will be selling.

resistance: bulls
and bears selling

support: bulls
and bears buying

Fig. A2-2

The concept of support and resistance is not limited to any market or any particular stock but rather is ubiquitous across markets. In Figure 2A-3 is shown a weekly chart of Sun Mircosystems (SUNW—NASDAQ), the network server company and developer of the Java technology. After its 1995-96 run-up in price to the mid 30s (pre-split price from 2000 levels), this stock experienced resistance to further price increases for about a year, trying unsuccessfully on several occasions to break though this level. At the same time it found price support around 28, which it also tested on several occasions. Once firm support and resistance levels such as these are formed, they become **channel lines**. The location of channel lines can be valuable knowledge for short-term traders,who will go long at the lower channel line and short at the upper channel line. Once channel lines are violated, however, prices can make a significant move in the direction of the violation. SUNW moved up nicely into the low $50 range once it broke through the 35 level in June 97.

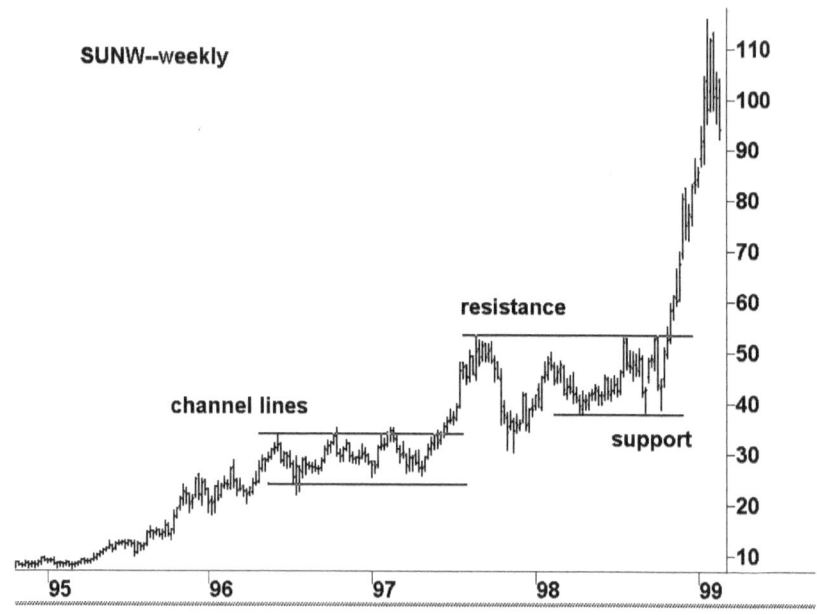

Fig. A2-3

For the remainder of 1997 and for much of 1998 this $50 level provided significant resistance to further price gains. Note that during this time support developed at around $38. Then finally in late 1998 SUNW made a big move up with the rest of the technology sector.

Trendlines and moving averages can also act as levels of support and resistance. In Figure A2-4 is shown a chart of Boeing (BA—NYSE), a world leader in aircraft manufacturing and a Dow Jones Industrials Average component. Superimposed on the price chart is a 40-week (200-day) moving average (MA). You can see in the steep rise from 1995 that this 40-week MA was tested on several occasions, but provided support each time in this rise to all-time highs for this stock.

Finally in mid to late 1997 and into early 1998 the support given by the 40-week moving average collapsed as a broad topping pattern formed. However, as Boeing's stock price declined further, the 40-week MA then turned into resistance as the stock began to build a base for a new leg up.

Fig. A2-4

I note that support and resistance levels take on more signifi-cance the longer prices remain at those levels and the more volume that takes place at those levels. Also, the most recent support and resistance levels typically take on greater signifi-cance because they are fresher in traders minds. However, it is always wise to be aware of where long resistance levels reside.

Round Numbers as Support and Resistance

Finally, support and resistance at round numbers can be crucial. It may seem ridiculous, but round numbers do influence speculators and investors alike. This can happen in stocks, bonds (usually the round number in this case is for yields, such as a 6% bond yield, etc.), currencies or precious metals. I give an example of this in the case of precious metals, where round numbers seem to take on a special significance. In Fig. 5 is shown a weekly chart of the spot gold price from its move up to the $400/ounce level in late 1993. You can see how that level was approached on several occasions, but continued to act as resistance. When the gold price declined sharply into 1998, the $300/ounce price level became resistance as can be seen on the bottom right of the chart.

Fig. A2-5

Changing Roles

Support and resistance levels can change roles, but only after one of these levels has been penetrated significantly. The question of what represents "significant" depends to some extent on the market in question as well as other factors. John Murphy in his excellent book, *Technical Analysis of the Futures Markets* (which is an excellent reference for technical analysis in general, not just for the futures markets) suggests that chartists use as a benchmark a 10% penetration as a criteria for major support and resistance levels. He further suggests that shorter-term support and resistance areas require smaller penetrations of from 3 to 5%. I suggest that this percent penetration depends on the particular market, be it gold, the Swiss franc or the stock of Intel. As always, it is prudent to be familiar with the past price action of any prospective investment. Also the price level can be important. A 2-point penetration move of a conservative $20 stock can be more important than a 7-point penetration move of a volatile $70 stock.

To understand the psychology of how support and resistance change roles, let's take the price action of gold as an example. First consider the thinking of gold bulls (i.e., those *long* the market). As gold falls to, say, $300/ounce, they are confident that the price will hold and they increase their positions. In fact, it is quite likely that even traders with no strong convictions on the direction of gold will buy at this price, since $300 is a well-known support level. Finally gold bears (those who are *short* the market) take profits in this area by buying back their positions, because they, too, are aware of the strong psychological support at $300. So, in other words, at the $300-level for gold, bulls, recently committed speculators and bears are all buying. This is what constitutes a support area.

Now, for whatever reason, be it announcements of central banks sales, or whatever, gold does not hold at $300, but drops to $290. Suddenly the bulls and recently committed speculators are sitting on losing positions and the bears are crying in their beer because they closed out their positions too soon. As gold tries to climb back to the $300 level, the bulls and speculators will liquidate positions in order to break even on their trades. Bears will initiate new short positions because they missed out on the down move below $300 the first time around. Now, at the former support level, bulls, speculators and bears are all selling. This constitutes a resistance level. Thus, a support level has turned into resistance.

Without giving a detailed example, it should be clear that resistance can equally well turn into support. Just turn the gold example in the last paragraph around with gold surging through the $300 level.

I depend heavily on support and resistance in my trading and in the recommendations made in my newsletter, *The Whole Investor Report*. With the explanations above, you now understand that these levels are not just lines on a chart, but that they actually impact the psychology of traders. We want to be able to understand that psychology and take advantage of it.

Investing Discipline

A discussion of support and resistance levels leads naturally into one of the *most important aspects of money management as applied to investing*: **set limits when you first make an investment on how much you are willing to lose—then stick by that decision.** Get out of that investment when it reaches a 10% loss or a 15% loss or perhaps when it drops 5% past a known support level—whatever your level of tolerance is. **Get** out fast without hesitation. *Discipline is the key*. I have convinced myself in recent years that the maximum loss on any stock should never be more than 15%, but I have increasingly begun to trade off support and resistance levels with loss limits from such levels of 5-7%. Never fall in love and "get married" to any investment. That is the way 10-15% losses become 50% losses.

We also need a corollary to the above money management rule. The corollary applies to those cases when we show a gain in our position. Basically the rule involves how much of that gain we are willing to give back. Markets and investment prices do not go in one direction. They spurt, zigzag and stall. You have to give some investments more room to maneuver than others. Nevertheless, **you must set limits on how much of a retracement of your investment gains you will tolerate**. Typically I allow a larger percentage for retracements on gains than I would allow for an investment loss. But establishing a firm rule for retracements can prove tricky.

Suppose you have a 3-point gain on a 20-dollar stock. One day some analyst puts the kibosh on the company and the stock price promptly falls 1¾ points. Do you sell? Probably not. These are situations where support and resistance levels can be particularly useful. Suppose you buy a 20-dollar stock that spurts to 28, then falls back to a support level at 25 and sits there a few days. The next day, some analyst puts the kibosh on the company and the stock price falls 1¾ points. Do you sell? Yes. A 7% fall through a support level is more important than a larger trading retracement from a near term high. I know—the self-recriminations will follow. Oh, I could have sold the stock at 28, and here I am with a lousy 3-point gain rather than an 8-point gain, etc., etc. But that's the wrong kind of thinking. You did the right thing and you knew what you were doing. Chances are a few days or weeks later the stock price will be under where you bought it originally. I rarely get out at the top in any investment. Neither do most professional traders. Use support/resistance levels and percent retracements. Those who believe they can do better on a consistent basis are engaging in fortune-telling, not investing.

One last money management rule that I've personally found useful is: **never tolerate a losing position on an investment in which you've once had a gain.** This one requires a surprising amount of discipline. It can occur in a matter of a couple of days and usually is a bit of a shock. Say you buy a $20-dollar stock that goes up 1½ the first day, and you are quite pleased with your alacrity. The next day the price falls 2-points, and you are left gasping for breath. Get out. Admit a defeat. In the long term you will be pleasantly surprised with the usefulness of this rule.

References

1. John Murphy, *Technical Analysis of the Futures Markets*, New York Institute of Finance, New York, NY, 1986.

2. Martin J. Pring, *Technical Analysis Explained*, McGraw-Hill, New York, NY, 1991

3. Dr. Alexander Elder, *Trading for a Living*, John Wiley & Sons, New York, NY, 1993.

Special Offer To Readers Of The Amazing Common Sense Guide For Your Investment Success

Send for a **free issue** of *THE WHOLE INVESTOR REPORT*. This timely financial newsletter appeals to those investors who find it prudent to broadly diversify their portfolios, who enjoy keeping abreast of financial market developments, and who wish to continue learning about various aspects of investment.

With the volatility in various markets around the world, the value of the "Whole Investing" approach is fast becoming apparent.

Ten times a year, *THE WHOLE INVESTOR REPORT* gives updates on the **equity markets**, the **debt markets**, the **currency markets** and the **precious metals markets**. Enjoy at your leisure the **INCREASE YOUR INVESTMENT KNOWLEDGE** section, where investors can learn important techniques to improve investing performance, or the **BOOK REVIEW** of important works in investing, the economy or finance. No other financial newsletter provides the diversification or learning possibilities that *THE WHOLE INVESTOR REPORT* does. Why not try a free copy?

___Yes, I want to take advantage of this special offer for *The Whole Investor Report*. Please send my free issue to the address below.

___Please sign me up for a *3-issue* trial subscription to *The Whole Investor Report* for only **$10**. My check made out to **WHOLE INVESTOR FINANCIAL RESEARCH** is enclosed.

___I prefer to subscribe immediately to *The Whole Investor Report* for one year at the special rate of **$79.**

Please print all information:

Name_____

Address_____

City_____State_____ZIP Code_____

Please send to:

        Whole Investor Financial Research
        165 N. Hills Place
        State College, PA 16803

www.ingramcontent.com/pod-product-compliance
Lightning Source LLC
Chambersburg PA
CBHW030920180526
45163CB00002B/408